TEACHING
COMPUTERS
TO
TEACH

TEACHING COMPUTERS TO TEACH

Esther R. Steinberg

*Computer-based Education Research
Laboratory and College of Education
University of Illinois at Urbana-Champaign*

 LAWRENCE ERLBAUM ASSOCIATES, PUBLISHERS
1984   Hillsdale, New Jersey   London

Copyright © 1984 by Lawrence Erlbaum Associates, Inc.
All rights reserved. No part of this book may be reproduced in
any form, by photostat, microform, retrieval system, or any other
means, without the prior written permission of the publisher.

Lawrence Erlbaum Associates, Inc., Publishers
365 Broadway
Hillsdale, New Jersey 07642

Library of Congress Cataloging in Publication Data

Steinberg, Esther R.
 Teaching computers to teach.

 Bibliography: p.
 Includes index.
 1. Computer-assisted instruction—Computer programs.
I. Title.
LB1028.5.S73 1984   371.3'9445   83-25428
ISBN 0-89859-368-9
     0-89859-453-7 (Pbk.)

Printed in the United States of America
10 9 8 7 6 5 4 3 2 1

To Marvin —

My husband, my friend.

Contents

Preface

This book is designed for people who want to learn how to develop computer-assisted instruction (CAI). It should serve both individuals who have taught but have never designed instruction and those who have designed instruction other than CAI. Those who have programmed computers but have neither taught nor developed instruction will learn how to apply their expertise to a new field. The product of several years of classroom testing, this volume has proven its value as a textbook for courses in the design of computer-presented lessons.

The purpose of this book is to present procedures and principles for designing instruction delivered by computer. The reader will learn what to do, how to do it, and why it should be done in a particular way. The implications for programming the computer are discussed but programming per se is not.

The procedures and principles recommended are based on two themes. The first is that the learner is the focus of CAI. The production of the lesson is guided by the learners' knowledge, skills, understanding, expectations, and motivation. The learners' educational needs, not the computer hardware or software, determine the nature of the lesson. The second theme is that the computer is neither instruction nor a method of instruction; it is merely a vehicle of instruction. The computer offers powerful features for facilitating learning, such as tutor-like interaction with the learner. However, a lesson is effective only when these features are properly applied. These two themes are fundamental to generating quality CAI regardless of the type of computer used.

A consequence of this philosophy is that many components must be considered in order to produce CAI: the subject matter presentation, the interactive dialogue between computer and learners, smooth communication between learners and the computer, monitoring learners' understanding, motivating learners, sequencing the flow of instruction, designing screen displays, programming the computer, and evaluating the lesson. Since it is difficult to attend to all of these aspects of lesson development simultaneously, the author needs a systematic procedure for managing the components. The Three-Phase Plan, embracing the Ripple Plan, is such a procedure. The first seven chapters present this procedure, its components, and methods of implementing them. The order of the chapter content is the order in which the lesson is generated. A sample lesson, initiated in chapter 2 to illustrate the concepts presented, is carried along and developed in succeeding chapters until a unit of instruction is actually produced.

There are so many special considerations for generating drills, games, and simulations in CAI that a separate chapter is devoted to those topics. Finally, the last chapter discusses methods of making lesson production efficient and implementation effective.

The system for lesson production presented here is effective for producing lessons on both microcomputer systems and those controlled by a large central computer. The sample lesson in the text was generated on both the APPLE II and the PLATO systems.[1]

I wish to acknowledge the following individuals, who each in his or her own way have been instrumental in my professional growth: Richard C. Anderson, R. Allen Avner, Donald Bitzer, and Constance Curtin. Appreciation is also due Paul Tenczar for his critical reading of the manuscript and Dorothy Rosen for her able editorial assistance.

Esther R. Steinberg

---

[1]The PLATO® system is a development of the University of Illinois. PLATO® is a service mark of Control Data Corporation.

The word APPLE is a registered trademark of APPLE COMPUTER INC.

TEACHING COMPUTERS TO TEACH

1 Getting Oriented

INTRODUCTION

Good computer-assisted instruction (CAI) doesn't just happen; authors make it happen. The purpose of this book is to help them do so by presenting a set of principles, guidelines, and procedures for generating effective CAI.

Creating CAI is more than merely presenting content, designing displays, or managing technical matters. It entails an understanding of how CAI differs from traditional modes of instruction and how this difference affects the nature of the instructional presentation. The author must be a subject matter expert, a tutor, a psychologist, a lesson designer, an evaluator, and a display artist.

When generating CAI lessons, the author combines knowledge about computers with a knowledge of teaching and instructional design, while remaining cognizant of the unique aspects of human-machine interaction. Expertise in all of these disciplines is, however, only one facet of design. It is the salient reorganizing, blending, and adapting of all this information that produces effective CAI.

You, the author, plan the interaction: design the questions, anticipate students' responses, and provide appropriate feedback. You create dynamic effects in individual displays, retaining one part of a display while erasing other parts, and making diagrams "grow" step by step while engaging learners in an interactive dialogue about what's happening. You decide who will control the learning: the student, the computer, the classroom instructor, or some combination of these. You write the computer program and eventually produce the final product, the lesson the learners will actually use.

What makes a CAI lesson effective? Students do not necessarily acquire desired skills and processes just because the lesson is presented by a computer. Boring lessons do not maintain students' attention in CAI any more than in traditional instruction. Games and entertaining activities may not be instructionally effective even though they do maintain students' attention. Even innovative lessons, such as simulations of physical phenomena, may not produce insights about those phenomena, particularly if the presentation is not geared to the student's level of knowledge.

Similarly, lessons are not automatically effective because they are presented on a particular CAI system, whether it is a self-contained microcomputer system or one controlled by a large central computer. The computer itself is only the medium of instruction; it is no better than the lesson it presents. Good lessons require lucid presentations, stimulating questions, helpful feedback, and effective graphics, regardless of the type of computer employed. Poor lessons — such as repetitive drills — are no more effective on a powerful system than on a small one.

Creating an effective lesson involves making a plan and following a systematic procedure for implementing, evaluating, and revising it. Some aspects of lesson development must be planned for the lesson as a whole; others are more reasonably developed for individual parts of the instruction, because they cannot be readily predetermined or because a single set of decisions is not appropriate for the entire lesson.

Therefore, the procedure is to plan and produce the lesson at two levels: (1) the overall lesson and (2) the instructional subsections (units of instruction). Do the initial planning at the overall lesson level, then generate the units of instruction and finally complete production at the overall lesson level. A brief overview of this Three-Phase Plan follows.

At the lesson level, formulate the overall goals and plan measures to ascertain whether the learners have reached those goals. Analyze the task to determine both the subject matter knowledge and the learning strategies students must acquire to accomplish the goals. Planning also includes management and human factors decisions about the lesson as a whole. For instance, decide which keys should be assigned special functions; that is, which keys a learner will press to "tell" the computer that she wants to review a display or return to the table of contents. Every lesson must have introductory and concluding displays, such as a title page and a final message indicating the end of the lesson. Finally, no plans are complete until they include formal procedures for evaluating and revising the lesson. There is no way of knowing how well a lesson functions until it is tested with the students for whom it was written.

Clearly, it is not possible to complete all planning at the lesson level before beginning work at the unit level. It makes no sense to make decisions on lesson management or to design a table of contents before formulating and producing the instruction that needs to be managed. Therefore, after initial planning of some of the components, such as specifying goals and analyzing the task, proceed to the instructional unit level.

Using the task analysis as a guide, divide the lesson into units and work on one unit at a time. Formulate the presentation: compose the explanations, the examples and the graphics to illustrate the points. Plan the interaction: write the questions, the acceptable responses and the feedback for the various responses. Plan the flow of instruction within the unit for the smoothest possible learner-computer interaction. After planning the unit, produce it for presentation on the computer, try it out, and then make necessary revisions.

In order to manage all of these aspects of developing the units, follow the procedure called the Ripple Plan. The basic idea is to generate one component at a time, rather than trying to develop all components of the unit (presentation, responses and feedback, human factors and management) simultaneously. Produce one component and evaluate it, in order to determine the revisions needed, before going on to the next component.

After the units of instruction are generated, evaluated, and revised, focus on completing the overall lesson. This is the time to make decisions on overall lesson management, as well as to design and produce the introductory and concluding displays. Finally, test and revise the entire product until it is ready for use.

When creating CAI, try to use the computer's capabilities in the most advantageous ways. To do so, become acquainted with the computer as an instructional medium. Learn how it differs from other media. Review available CAI lessons. The sections that follow present: (1) a discussion of the differences between CAI and other instructional modes and the implications for designing CAI, (2) a rationale for the necessity of reviewing available CAI lessons, and (3) a procedure for lesson review.

DIFFERENCES BETWEEN CAI AND TRADITIONAL MODES OF INSTRUCTION

Human-machine Interaction

The most obvious difference between CAI and classroom instruction is that in CAI the human is interacting with a machine rather than with another human being. The dynamics of communication are different. In the classroom, only one person answers each question posed by the instructor, while others sit and listen. Some choose to respond as little as possible, and others monopolize the answering. In CAI, every student can be required to respond to every question: no daydreaming while others in the class come up with answers! Some students do not respond in the classroom because they are afraid of being wrong and being embarrassed or ridiculed by the others. In CAI, learners answer in the privacy of their interaction with the computer terminal.

Students can ask questions in many ways in the classroom and expect the instructor to understand them. Only a few CAI lessons have such capabilities, and these are limited in the breadth of questioning allowed. Instructors can accept all correct answers, whatever their form, whether anticipated or not. The answer to the question, "Who was the first president of the United States?" may be "Washington," "George Washington," or "Washington was the first president." The teacher will understand and accept as correct every one of these responses. In CAI the lesson has to be designed to do so. In the future, computers may be able to understand natural language, but at present this capability is still the subject of intensive research.

CAI is usually an individual activity, and thus the benefits of group discussion are lacking. In the classroom, students can learn from one another's responses as well as from the instructor. In CAI the lesson itself is the only source of information.

The mode of communication is different in the classroom, where students receive information both orally and visually: they hear and they see. When students are to follow a set of written directions, teachers sometimes read the directions aloud to the class and explain them in greater detail. Even when students are expected to read the directions by themselves, they can ask the teacher for clarification, if necessary. In contrast, in CAI most directions are currently transmitted visually: students see but do not hear. They depend only on reading text and interpreting graphics to find out what to do.

In the classroom the instructor can monitor a student's comprehension both by asking questions and by observing the student's behavior. The instructor can tell from a puzzled look or a hand in the air that a learner does not understand. The computer cannot see the student. A CAI lesson can assess a student's understanding only by asking pertinent questions and monitoring responses. A classroom instructor can also see when a student is no longer paying attention. Looking out of the window, dropping pencils, and staring vacantly into space are all visual cues not available to the computer.

In the classroom students usually respond by speaking or writing on paper or blackboard. In CAI they do neither. In CAI students respond most frequently by pressing keys on a typewriter-like keyset or, less frequently, by touching a specially designed display screen or even pressing a button on a paddle.

These differences between classroom learning and CAI greatly affect the responsibilities of the lesson designer. Directions must be particularly precise and understandable because the student will not necessarily have a human to turn to for further explanation. If the lesson does provide supplementary instruction or practice exercises, the display must communicate that information to the student, informing him (1) that more information is available and (2) how to access it. For example, the message might be, "Press Key E for additional examples." Interaction is an absolute essential in CAI. The lesson has to ask questions and judge responses in order to monitor students' progress as well as to maintain their attention. The computer lesson must be designed to accept as nearly as possible all correct answers and reject all incorrect ones. The designer must enable the learner to communicate easily with the machine, by, for example, minimizing the amount of typing required.

Individualization

Another characteristic of CAI is that it is individually paced, in contrast to traditional classroom instruction, which is group-paced. In group instruction, even small-group instruction, a student who does not understand a concept must move along with the rest of the class although not ready to do so. A student who learns quickly must sit and wait for the others. Not so in CAI. Each student can work at an appropriate level of difficulty and proceed in the lesson at a pace that it appropriate for him. If a student finds a concept troublesome, remedial sequences and extra practice are available. A student who learns quickly does not have to waste time listening to repetitions of material already learned.

Such individualized instruction is a hallmark of CAI, but it does not occur automatically. It is the author of the lesson who makes it happen for the learner.

Decisions

The CAI author must make instructional and managerial decisions that are not an issue in other media. A textbook author may insert questions or problems in the book but does not have to decide how many questions the student should answer. The student or the instructor decides. The CAI author does have control and must decide not only how many questions to ask, but whether to force the student to answer them and whether to require a given level of mastery before allowing the student to proceed. Clearly, the author has many more decisions to make than how to present the lesson content.

Pedagogical, design, managerial, and production decisions – ALL must be made BEFORE the learner studies the lesson. A classroom instructor can decide at the moment of instruction what to say if a student gives a wrong answer. That strategy won't work for a CAI lesson. The author must make such decisions during the planning stage. Decisions can be revised if student trials of the lesson indicate the need, but they must be made before the lesson is actually used for instruction.

Data Keeping

Tests, homework, and classroom worksheets provide the evaluation data in traditional instruction. These data are usually used to evaluate the student's performance and overall class performance. They may be used to evaluate instruction, but in practice this usage rarely occurs. In CAI, data are used to evaluate the lesson while it is being developed as well as to manage the learner's instructional path, and to report on both individual student and overall class performance. For example, during lesson testing a record is kept of learners' incorrect responses. This record enables the author to revise the lesson in order to provide feedback specific to those incorrect responses. Suppose, for example, that task is to write the names of the months, given the abbreviations. The data show that common incorrect spellings for February are "february" and "Febuary." Rather than responding only No to all errors, the lesson can be revised to say either "Names of months are capitalized" or "You have left out a letter."

Time to Develop CAI Lessons

In addition to all these aspects of lesson design, CAI involves actually producing the lesson, designing the graphic display, and programming the computer. Consequently, generating a lesson, particularly the first one, takes an enormous amount of time. The time varies with a number of factors: the complexity of the lesson, whether the author works independently or with others, and whether the lesson makes use of an existing CAI teaching strategy or generates a new one. Group-paced classroom pedagogical techniques rarely transfer well to CAI. Therefore, considerable time is required to generate techniques appropriate for individualized, computer-presented instruction. After one or two lessons, the time needed to produce CAI lessons usually decreases and then levels off. Production time may increase again if a subsequent lesson involves some innovative or complex design.

The first lesson that you author will demand a heavy investment of time at the outset. Generating CAI lessons is so complex that unless you devote a concentrated mass of time at the beginning, you will find yourself forgetting what you did previously and spending too much time whenever you return to the task, repeating what you did earlier.

Feasibility of Innovative Instruction

CAI provides would-be authors with the opportunity of developing an entirely new approach to instruction. The lesson may simulate a real-life situation. It may enable students to "step through" procedures so that they are better prepared when they encounter the real task later. For example, a lesson can enable a student nurse to simulate monitoring a patient in labor. The student must make decisions and experience the consequences.

Psychology of CAI Lesson Designers

A special set of attitudes evolve as authors design CAI lessons. They become personally involved in their lessons and take pride in them, just as artists do in their paintings. Authors have invested so much time and so much of themselves in the lesson that they naturally dislike negative reviews of their "creation." Beginning authors, in particular, tend to be very defensive about that first lesson and find it difficult to accept criticism. They can alleviate this situation by asking colleagues and students to appraise the lesson while it is being developed. It should help beginners to know that first lessons are generally not outstanding. Even an experienced author rarely writes an excellent lesson without some revisions. During student trials or peer reviews it is not uncommon for an author to wonder, "How could I do such a dumb thing?"

Beginning authors tend to become enamored of CAI and try to see how creative they can be. They include every feature of the computer system, even if it does not improve the lesson or actually detracts from it. For example, they design cute little characters to move across the screen, though the graphics neither motivate nor facilitate learning; such graphics may bore or slow down the student if they occur too frequently in the lesson. Authors may err by using many attention-getting techniques simultaneously, thus defeating the purpose of drawing attention to the critical feature on the display. For instance, they may use several colors, frames around words, text in several sizes and flashing, all at the same time. The author must be wary not to misuse the computer's capabilities.

Inexperienced authors find it helpful to work in close communication with individuals who are experienced in CAI, whose encouragement and advice enable the beginner to make better progress. Such aid is particularly helpful if the beginning lesson designer is simultaneously learning a programming language. A programming consultant can guide the beginner over difficult spots and indicate which parts of the programming language the author should learn first.

RATIONALE AND GUIDELINES FOR REVIEWING CAI LESSONS

Reasons for Reviewing Lessons

Before you begin designing CAI lessons, take time to review lessons that others have written. Even if you have previously seen or done CAI lessons, review some others.

Why review such lessons? First you, as a CAI author, need to know what it is like to be a student studying in the CAI mode. Nearly everybody has had the experience of being a student in a traditional classroom. Everybody remembers that some teachers and some learning experiences were outstanding; others were boring or mediocre, at best. The reasons for these feelings were varied. Good teachers were outstanding because they made the subject matter relevant or because they were patient with a student's particular learning problems. A class was boring because the pace of instruction was geared to the slower students. In contrast to this universal experience, most people have not studied in the CAI mode and have no experience to recall, either good or bad. They have not enjoyed the satisfaction and delight of the computer's immediate report of how much their performance has improved. On the other hand, they have not undergone the frustration of sitting in front of a terminal and finding that they cannot proceed because the directions are unclear and there is no human instructor to turn to.

The entire human-machine interaction is different from other learning experiences. It is difficult to appreciate the impact of this difference on a student unless you have experienced human-machine interaction directly. The value of such experience should not be underestimated.

Reviewing CAI lessons will also help in finding out what lessons are already available. This review will be useful for two reasons: (1) to avoid wasting time repeating work that has already been done and (2) to get ideas of work that needs to be done. There is no need to reinvent the wheel. If lessons are available and suitable for your students and your curriculum, why not use them? If a lesson only partially fulfills a need, it can still serve as a basis for writing a revised and expanded version. Even a lesson in a different subject matter area may demonstrate useful techniques that can be incorporated or adapted for your lessons. Available lessons may even inspire entirely new ideas for using CAI in ways you had not thought about.

Whether or not you have reviewed some CAI lessons in the past, seek out current lessons to review. Computer technology is changing so fast that there will be rapid advances and innovations in CAI lessons, too. For example, find out how lessons are incorporating color and sound in CAI.

Working through CAI lessons as a student will make you more cognizant of the differences between classroom teaching and CAI. You will become aware of the many facets of instruction that must be considered in designing CAI and will realize that instructional design is more than presenting content or managing technical aspects.

Those who have already designed instruction, such as programmed instruction, may not realize how it differs from CAI. There are intrinsic differences, some of them unique to printed materials and others unique to CAI. Printed materials have some important characteristics that are not automatically available in CAI, but must be designed. We are so accustomed to these printed, text-like materials that we take for granted some of the ways they are used in learning. Getting around in the material is one example. The student can flip back a page or two to review, or flip forward to the end of the lesson if he chooses to do so. This option is implicit in printed materials. However, moving around in the lesson freely is not an intrinsic feature of CAI; the lesson author must arrange it. On the other hand, CAI possesses characteristics not usually present in programmed instruction, such as the capability of forcing the student to respond before he can see or look up the correct answer.

Guidelines for Reviewing Lessons

Lessons are written for a particular group of students, designated as the target population. This population may be a large and general group, such as adults, or special groups, such as third-graders who read at sixth-grade level. Of course, students from any population may try a CAI lesson, but the target population is the one for whom it is specifically designed by the author.

Keep in mind three features that are basic to all reviews:

1. A review includes description first, to be followed by evaluation; both are essential.

2. A review requires more than one pass through the lesson because CAI involves interaction and multiple instructional paths. An initial pass is necessary to get an overview and to describe the lesson as a whole. Additional passes enable you to assess specific features in detail. For example, use the second pass to determine whether the lesson asks questions to monitor the student's understanding or if it is essentially display after display of information, like a book. Ascertain whether supplementary instruction is available for a student who makes many errors. The number of passes needed depends on the complexity of the lesson. Plan on at least two passes.

3. Evaluation is relative rather than absolute. This precept leads to the following:

CARDINAL PRINCIPLE: Judge the design of the lessons for their consistency with objectives and their suitability for the target population.

Reviewers sometimes misjudge CAI lessons because they fail to abide by this principle. Suppose, for instance, that the author states that a lesson was written as an introduction to science for beginning high-school students. The author includes only general statements, such as: Water freezes at 32°F. The author does not mention exceptions, like the fact that water freezes at a lower temperature when it contains salt or sugar. It would be a mistake to reject the lesson on the grounds that the content is inadequate and states only half-truths. Such an evaluation would be appropriate if the lesson were intended for an advanced course. However, it was written for a beginning course and the content should be evaluated for its merits on that basis.

One further word of caution: There is a serious limitation to evaluating a lesson when you are not a member of the target population. It is difficult to imagine yourself as a fourth-grader doing an arithmetic lesson. A lesson that is boring to you may be interesting to the child; conversely, a lesson that you find fascinating and challenging may be of little interest to that child. As will be shown, evaluation entails perceptive observation of members of the target population.

PROCEDURES FOR REVIEWING LESSONS

The following procedures include the major components of lesson review and a method for executing them. As you gain experience you may wish to modify some of the details, such as the order in which to describe the components of the lesson.

First Pass — Components

The first pass has the same purpose as flipping through a book: to get an overview of the lesson and a general reaction to it. The goal in this first pass is to describe the lesson and to evaluate it in a general way.

Identification. The first component of the description is identification: the title, name(s) of the author(s), the date of publication or most recent revision and copyright information.

Content. Next, subject matter content is specified, including both the general subject area and the specific subarea. For example, the general subject may be the Pascal programming language, while the subarea is the structure of the Pascal language.

Boundary conditions. Another part of the description is a group of items termed *boundary conditions*: the target population, the goals of the lesson, and the role of the lesson in the larger course or curriculum.

Continuing with the example of the Pascal lesson, the target populations are first- and second-year students in two-year or four-year colleges. The goal is for learners to use correct structure when writing a Pascal program. The lesson is one of a series of lessons on Pascal, intended as practice to supplement primary instruction provided elsewhere.

Instructional techniques.   The description identifies the instructional technique(s) employed. If the lesson is direct instruction, a dialogue between computer and learner, it is called a tutorial. A tutorial lesson is basically a "tell and ask," in which information is presented, questions are asked, responses are given, and feedback is provided. If a lesson is practice in rote information, such as the memorizing of French vocabulary, it is a drill. If the lesson is practice in applying concepts or rules, like problem solving or applying rules of grammar, it is a practice lesson. Other kinds of lessons are simulations and games. These categories are not mutually exclusive. A drill may have a game format and a simulation may be both a drill and a game. In addition, a lesson may include more than one instructional technique, such as both tutorial and practice. In the Pascal lesson, note that the lesson explains concepts and asks questions to monitor the learner's understanding, and is, therefore, a tutorial lesson.

Technical matters.   Technical matters are reviewed in the first pass. The lesson must tell the learner how to communicate with the computer on matters such as which keys to press to move forward or backward. This information should be displayed where the learner will notice it and not be embedded in a cluttered display filled with "wall-to-wall" text. The Pascal lesson displays the message at the bottom of the screen: Press "RETURN" to continue, "*B*" to go back to the table of contents.

Supplementary equipment.   Some lessons require special equipment such as a color monitor; others require devices or materials in addition to standard CAI equipment. Workbooks may be needed to accompany CAI simulations. Lessons for nonreaders may require audio equipment such as tape recorders or audio disks. Such supplementary equipment should be mentioned in the description.

First Pass — Procedure

Since the objective of the first pass is to get a global view of the lesson, scan the whole lesson before describing it. First, "read in" the lesson; that is, get the computer to prepare the lesson for presentation. As the computer is preparing the lesson, notice whether the screen is blank or a message is displayed. When the lesson is ready, proceed through the introductory displays. The content of these displays will obviously vary from one lesson to another, but there should be a title page. Other displays might be a statement of purpose, a table of contents, or rules for playing if the lesson is a game. If there is a table of contents, select the first item to sample first; proceed through a few displays to get the general idea, and then return to the table of contents and sample some other items. If the lesson has no table of contents, continue on past the introductory displays and go far enough into the lesson so that you can describe and evaluate it in terms of the items noted above. These items are summarized in Fig. 1.1. Use it as a guide in the initial pass.

Note that some of the information you are seeking in the first pass may not be given on-line (on the computer), but rather off-line. Items such as the target population, the purpose of the lesson, and the implementation within the curriculum may be available only in a brochure that accompanies the lesson. If the lesson you are reviewing is one of a series, such information may be presented only in the initial lesson. There are lessons for which some of this information may not be available at all.

After you have completed the first pass, write the review. If some of the identifying information (for example, the target population) is not provided by the lesson publishers, make a note of what is lacking and infer what the information might be. In addition to describing the lesson, give an overall reaction to it. Note the outstanding features, both good and bad, including motivational, creative or innovative elements. An outstanding feature in the Pascal lesson is that the organization of the lesson and the student's location in it are apparent at all times. The current topic of instruction (for example, variable declarations) is always shown in large print at the top of the display.

The first pass is only a start on reviewing the instructional design and does not provide enough detail to predict the potential effectiveness of the lesson or its suitability for the target population. The purpose of the next pass(es) is to examine in greater depth the presentation and the overall lesson management. Your ability to make judgments will depend on your familiarity with the content and whether you have taught it in an interactive mode (in contrast to straight lecture) to the target population. If you are unfamiliar with the content of the lesson, or know the content but have never taught it interactively to the target population, you will only be able to implement the recommendations partially. For example, you can see which topics are covered, but lack a basis for judging the accuracy or adequacy of the content for the designated learners. Try to find lessons in areas you have taught, in order to do a full review of the lesson.

Second Pass — Components

The second pass through the lesson is the time to examine five broad categories in detail: content, instructional techniques, lesson management, human factors, and displays (Fig. 1.2).

```
Review of an Individual Lesson
The First Pass: Overview

Identification

    Title
    Author(s)
    Date of publication or most recent revision
    Copyright

Content

    General area
    Subarea

Boundary conditions

    Purpose
    Target population
    Designated implementation

Instructional techniques

    Tutorial
    Drill: Rote memory
    Practice: Problem solving, applications
    Game
    Simulation

Technical

    Entering, exiting, getting around in lesson
    Knowing how to enter responses
    Aesthetics

Supplementary equipment required

    Color monitor
    Touch devices
    Audio devices
    Workbooks, guidelines
    Other

Overall reaction

    Strongest point(s)
    Weakest point(s)
    Motivational features
    Creative or innovative features
```

FIG. 1.1   Items to be considered during the first pass when reviewing the instructional design of a CAI lesson.

Review of an Individual Lesson
Second and Succeeding Passes

Content

   Prerequisite skills
   Topics covered — adequacy
   Accuracy

Instructional techniques

   Presentation

      Concise, unambiguous
      Hints on learning strategies
      Graphics consistent with text

   Questions

      Types: Open-ended, multiple-choice, match, true-false
      Frequency
      Require processing of presentation
      Relevant to content

   Responses

      Required?
      Flexible response judging

   Feedback and remediation

      Function of feedback
      Availability of remediation

Lesson management

   Algorithms for proceeding through the lesson
   Locus of control — Learner, teacher, computer

Human factors

   Interacting with the computer

      Student knows what to expect
      Consistency in use of keys
      No blind alleys
      Getting around in the lesson

   Motivation

   Displays

      Uncluttered
      Aesthetics

FIG. 1.2   Items to be considered during the second and succeeding passes when reviewing the instructional design of a CAI lesson.

Content.   First, examine the content, noting the topics covered. Are they consistent with the purpose of the lesson and the designated implementation? Are all the essential topics included? Are inappropriate topics included? While reviewing the content, note the prerequisite skills and knowledge the learner will need specifically for this lesson. For example, to do a lesson on the structure of the Pascal programming language, the learner must know the Pascal arithmetic operations. Evaluate the suitability of the prerequisites for the specified target population. Can the target population be expected to have these skills? The answer is yes for the hypothetical Pascal lesson; the learners are expected to do the lesson on Pascal arithmetic before starting the present one.

Check for content accuracy. Surprising as it may be, at the current state of the art many CAI lessons contain content errors. The errors may be actual misinformation, such as incorrect translation of a foreign vocabulary, or information that is out of date, such as census information or the names of government officials.

Instructional techniques.   When considering instructional techniques, evaluate the quality of the presentations. Are they concise or needlessly wordy and chatty? Are they understandable? Do they cover the full range of the particular concept, so that a student can learn all its aspects without mistakenly including assumptions that are not part of the concept? If the lesson is a game, are the directions sufficiently clear to play the game or do the learners have to puzzle out what they are supposed to do? If diagrams or animations are included, are they relevant to the instruction? If the subject matter is complex for the target population, are hints provided to help the student learn the content? For example, if a complex diagram is shown, is there a verbal explanation to point out those parts of the diagram that exemplify the concept?

Questions and responses are an essential part of CAI. Note the types of questions; they may be a form of recognition, such as multiple choice, true-false, or matching. They may require that the student recall or generate the answer by defining a concept or solving a problem. Notice how much "thinking" the student must do in order to answer. Does the student have to pay attention to the presentation to answer the questions, or can he copy the answers from another part of the display or give the correct answer on the basis of general knowledge? Are the questions relevant to the topic under discussion? Notice how frequently the student is asked to enter a response. Are questions asked often enough to maintain attention and to monitor understanding? (It is difficult to answer this last question unless you have observed students from the target population. This question is inserted to highlight its significance in lesson design.)

Response handling should be reviewed intensively. As a general rule, the student should be required to enter a response before seeing the correct one.

Allowing the learner to look at the correct answer before entering her own defeats the purpose of CAI as an individualized, interactive vehicle of instruction. Notice whether the computer accepts all reasonable responses. It must do so; the student should not have to guess the exact words the lesson author had in mind. If one correct response to a question is "fruits and vegetables," then the computer must also accept "vegetables and fruits."

In CAI, feedback refers to the information the computer gives after the student makes a response. The feedback may be as simple as yes or no; it may be as elaborate as an explanation of why the student's answer is incorrect. Judge feedback in terms of its value in helping the student meet lesson objectives.

Notice whether remediation is provided, and if so, what form it takes. The lesson might explain the material in a different way or provide additional examples. On the other hand, it might simply cycle the student through the same material.

Lesson management. In lesson management, an author decides on certain rules for allowing the student to proceed through the lesson and programs them into the computer. One rule may be that the student must answer at least 80% of the questions correctly in each section before she is allowed to go on to the next. Alternatively, the lesson may allow the classroom teacher to set the level of achievement, or the lesson may provide an index and allow the student total freedom of choice on which topics to study, and in what order. Some combination of computer-student control is a third alternative. In the lesson you are reviewing, describe the system used and judge its potential for success with the target population.

Human factors. Human factors include such matters as the student's awareness of what to do next, and his confidence that all necessary information will be provided. For example, he can always press a particular key if he needs to look up the rules of the game. There should be no blind alleys; that is, the student should not find himself at a point where he just cannot go on. The mechanics of entering and correcting a response must be readily understood by the student.

Displays. Finally, displays can make a difference in the effectiveness of a lesson. If a display is cluttered, a student may not notice some critical elements . If the main points are highlighted or emphasized in some way, the student will be more apt to notice them. Color and graphics should be employed in an instructionally significant way. If either or both are used, observe whether they foster learning or motivation. It is not the use of these features per se that is important, but how they are implemented.

Second Pass — Procedure

It is best to make two passes after the first, once to do the lesson without making deliberate errors, and once to make a lot of mistakes. Figure 1.2 summarizes items to be considered on passes after the first. Let us assume that you are doing three passes in all. The second pass addresses all of the items listed in Fig. 1.2, except remediation and certain aspects of algorithms needed for proceeding through the lesson. These last features are the focus of the third pass.

Third Pass

The best way to determine the rules for advancing the student through the lesson and also to review remediation and feedback is to pretend to be an unsuccessful learner. Three different ways of being unsuccessful produce different kinds of information: (1) For a given question, enter the same incorrect response at least twice. (2) Enter incorrect responses on successive questions. Answer one question after another incorrectly to find out if the lesson provides remediation, and under what conditions. For example, one lesson may provide remediation if the student scores less than 75% on an end-of-the-lesson quiz. Another lesson may branch the learner to supplementary instruction if he performs poorly during the lesson, perhaps answering half of the questions incorrectly on the first try. Some authors claim their lessons provide remediation, when in fact they simply force the learner to repeat the same instruction. Others present new instruction, adding different explanations or new examples. The latter method has a far greater probability of success than the former. (3) Try entering different incorrect responses for a given question. Make different kinds of errors to see whether the feedback is a standard reply to all errors or responsive to specific ones.

Postscript

Evaluations are done for a purpose; the nature of the evaluation is determined by that purpose. Since the evaluation is to assess the instructional design, only matters relating directly to design are suggested in these guidelines. If you were evaluating courseware for purchase, it would be necessary to gather additional information, such as the name of the computer system for which the lesson was available, computer memory requirements, and so on. The evaluation guidelines presented here are not intended to address such considerations.

2 Lesson Design: The Three-Phase Plan and the Ripple Plan

INTRODUCTION

A plan is essential to guide the production of CAI lessons. The Three Phase Plan, embracing the Ripple Plan, is a design procedure specifically for computer-presented instruction. The lesson must not only be planned; it must be programmed for the computer as well. Therefore, a discussion of whether you should learn a computer language well enough to do your own programming is presented at the end of the chapter.

What to Expect

As a beginning author, expect to spend a lot of time in developing CAI lessons and also in revising them. Lesson design is not a one-shot effort, even for experienced authors. No matter how much time you spend generating the lesson, you will still find it necessary to revise it, partly because you yourself will see ways to improve it and partly because trials with students and colleagues will point to changes that should be made for more effective instruction. Expect to be flexible, ready to think of alternative ways of presenting information, asking questions, and providing feedback.

Follow a Plan

Formulate and follow a plan for generating a lesson to increase the probability of reaching your goal, which is to develop a *finished* lesson. Novice designers sometimes lose sight of that goal. Rather, they get carried away with the medium, generating exciting displays and otherwise seeing what they can get the computer to do. They are not unlike the children in Fig. 2.1 who are cutting boards into shapes and sizes to see what they can create. Neither the children nor the designers know where their creativity will lead them. At best the children will be able to fit a few boards together to make some interesting designs. Novice lesson designers may create some flashy displays and perhaps a few instructional sequences. It is highly unlikely that they will produce a completed entity to show for all their efforts if they don't know exactly where they are going.

Generating a plan for instructional design is much like planning an automobile trip. You decide where you want to go, what route to take to get there, and what arrangements to make about needs, such as lodging. You do not simply get into your car and start driving, without knowing what route to take or making advance reservations. To do so could result in chaos. Similarly, generating a lesson requires a plan.

Creating a CAI lesson requires so many hours that it is important to waste as little time as possible. A plan can save time and make lesson production more efficient by avoiding aimless procedures. In the analogy of the vacationing motorist, there are many routes to a given destination. Some routes are shorter in distance but take more time because of poor

THE FAMILY CIRCUS®   **By Bil Keane**

7-11
Copyright 1981
The Register and Tribune
Syndicate, Inc.

"We don't know WHAT we're makin' yet. We just started."

FIG. 2.1   No plan, no goal, no predicting the outcome. (From *The Family Circus*. Copyright © 1981 by the Register and Tribune Syndicate, Inc. Reprinted by permission.)

roads or sections with low speed limits; other routes are longer in distance but takes less time because all of the driving can be done at high speed. Similarly, a lesson author can save time by planning ahead and giving consideration to all aspects of the design.

A plan enables you to respond in a systematic fashion to observed needs for changes. During implementation, the lesson may not function satisfactorily and will have to be revised. Having a plan to start with enables you to document the reason for the change. Such documenting will prevent you from subsequently making still another change that takes you back to the unsatisfactory starting point. The understanding gained from such systematic revision will thus broaden your base of knowledge about CAI lesson design.

Finally, a plan provides a standard against which to measure progress and can provide a background for future planning. A record of the time spent generating each component of the plan can serve as a basis for generating time lines for developing additional lessons.

THE THREE-PHASE PLAN

The three phases of the plan (Fig. 2.2) are (1) initial planning, (2) the Ripple Plan, and (3) completing the lesson. The first and third phases relate to the lesson as a whole, the middle phase to the individual units of instruction. Think of these phases as planning, producing, and putting it all together.

One of the strengths of the computer as a medium of instruction is that the author can see what the lesson looks like as soon as she finishes programming it. Thus, she can readily program any part of the instruction and immediately review it rather than wait until after the entire lesson is completed. This fast turnaround is exciting and exceedingly motivating. Unfortunately, it can be hazardous because it lends itself to composing at the terminal. That is, authors are frequently tempted to create bits of instruction while sitting at the computer terminal rather than making preliminary plans. While personally satisfying, this procedure is inefficient and often leads to an unfinished lesson or one that goes off on a tangent.

Both the Three-Phase Plan and its middle phase, the Ripple Plan, merge the benefits of the computer as the instructional vehicle with the requirements of sound instructional design principles. The essence of the Three-Phase Plan is (1) laying the groundwork for the lesson as a whole by making initial plans; (2) using these plans as a guide to produce the instruction one unit at a time; and (3) finally integrating the parts and completing the lesson.

As in instructional design for other media, initial planning is essential. The components of this first phase are characterizing the target population,

THE THREE-PHASE PLAN

I. Initial Planning: Lesson Level
    Characterize the target population.
    Formulate the overall goals.
    Analyze the task.
    Designate the prerequisite skills.
    Generate initial set of evaluation measures.

II. Ripple Plan: Unit Level
     Generate the presentation; program and evaluate.
     Expand response judging and feedback; program and evaluate.
     Make human factors and management decisions; program and evaluate.

III. Completing the Lesson: Lesson Level
      Complete management and human factors decisions.
      Generate introductory displays.
      Generate concluding displays.
      Complete initial set of evaluation measures.
      Evaluate and revise.
      Document.
      Plan maintenance.

FIG. 2.2   The Three-Phase Plan for generating computer-assisted instruction lessons.

formulating the overall goals, analyzing the task, designating the prerequisite skills, and generating an initial set of evaluation measures to assess student performance (Fig. 2.2).

After initial planning the author can choose either to create the entire lesson before programming it or to develop, program, and evaluate instruction, one section at a time. The latter method is preferable in CAI and is the procedure presented in the second phase of lesson development, the Ripple Plan. Unlike other media, CAI is interactive. The computer essentially carries on a dialogue with the learner and also manages the flow of instruction, contingent on that dialogue. The author generates the presentation, expands response judging and feedback, and makes human factors and management decisions. The author cannot predict what feedback to prepare for an entire lesson because he doesn't know which wrong answers learners will give or how much remediation they will require. Similarly, it is not reasonable to plan the complete flow of instruction before determining how students will perform. It is most efficient to produce and evaluate one unit at a time.

Finally, management and human factors decisions, such as criteria for advancing from one section to another or instructions to the student about how to study the lesson, are completed in the third phase of lesson development. Introductory and concluding displays are generated, the initial set of evaluation measures is completed, and the lesson as a whole is evaluated and documented. Plans are made for maintenance.

Notice that evaluation is not presented as a separate phase but rather as an integral part of every phase of lesson development. As will be shown, the purpose of evaluation varies from one phase to another: to measure lesson effectiveness during development, to monitor student performance while studying the lesson, and to measure student performance on completion of the lesson.

INITIAL PLANNING: LESSON LEVEL

Your function as the lesson author is to generate a lesson that helps students learn. To do so, you have to know who the learners are, what they are supposed to learn, and how you expect to use the computer to help them. In addition, measures must be prepared to determine whether learners achieve the lesson goals.

Target Population

The first step in initial planning is characterizing the group of learners for whom the lesson is designed, the target population. Begin by ascertaining the age or grade level and the level of learning skills, as well.

The instructional presentation will be different for learners of different ages even if the goals are the same for all. If the learners are adults in remedial English, different subject matter should be chosen to illustrate grammatical rules than if the learners are grade schoolers. To illustrate proper use of *who* to adult learners, an appropriate sentence is, "He is the man who repaired my car." For grade-school children a different context is more appropriate: "He is the man who took us to the zoo." Similarly, different presentations may be required for learners of the same age who have different learning skills. Hearing-impaired students, for example, lag behind in language and reading skills. Although they are at the same level in arithmetic, the sentence structure and vocabulary of the instruction must be different for them than for the hearing. Thus, it is important to characterize the target population by more than simply age or grade level. Specify the level of learning skills of the target population if the skills deviate from anticipated norms; for instance, the target learners are adults who read at fourth-grade level or sixth-graders who are hearing-impaired. If the target population is assumed to have some special training or education, state that information: The target population is second-year nursing students.

Overall Goals

The next step is generating the goals. In CAI there are three aspects to goal formulation: goals for the learner, the role of the computer in helping the learner achieve those goals, and the role of the lesson in the curriculum.

The reason for writing goals is to clarify in your own mind what the learners are supposed to accomplish. Goals provide a framework for designing the lesson as well as for evaluating it. This framework keeps you on course or alerts you to the need to change course. Consider, for example, instruction in the Russian language. If the goal is to translate scientific papers from Russian, the author of the CAI lessons will include Russian-to-English vocabulary drills. However, if the goal is to converse in Russian, then English-to-Russian vocabulary will be included, as well.

Learner goals.   The overall goal for the learner is a statement of the skills, knowledge, processes, or attitudes the learner will attain. The goal may be acquiring new knowledge like the concept of loops in computer programming, or maintaining or perfecting skills previously acquired, such as foreign-language vocabulary. The learner's goal may be applying rules or principles (for example, using pronouns correctly) or stepping through a decision-making process as a labor union leader would do in negotiating a union contract. Shaping or influencing the learner's attitude is yet another potential goal.

Beginning authors sometimes state learners' goals in such broad terms that the goals cannot realistically be achieved in a single CAI lesson. An example is the statement, "The student will learn to write an outline for term papers." So many topics would have to be addressed to achieve this goal that the lesson would be exceptionally long or would treat topics superficially, or perhaps include instruction not appropriate for CAI. Such a lesson would have little value for students. The author can avoid this situation by planning how the CAI lesson will fit into the curriculum and how the computer will fulfill the lesson goals. By defining the role of the computer and the role of the CAI lesson in the curriculum, the author will narrow the scope of the lesson to goals that are attainable in a single lesson. Further, there is a greater probability that the lesson will be studied if it serves a clearly defined purpose in the curriculum.

Role of the computer.   After stating the goals for the learner, it is essential to specify the role the computer will play toward achieving them. The diverse roles of the computer can be grouped into five broad categories: (1) providing individualization, (2) providing experience not otherwise possible, (3) separating practice in interdependent skills, (4) enabling curriculum revision, and (5) providing group interaction.

If the goals of the lesson are to improve rote knowledge or skill in well-defined procedures, as in arithmetic computation, CAI is often selected because the computer can be programmed to accommodate individual differences. CAI provides supplementary drills in environments where the practice in the classroom is not sufficiently individualized. For example, arithmetic programs are available to pretest students and place them at an appropriate knowledge and difficulty level. Each student drills on problems that are neither too easy nor too hard for him, as determined by a prespecified criterion. The computer advances each student upward through the program according to his own performance.

In some subjects the goal is to solve problems by applying rules and principles. In complex tasks of this sort, some students misunderstand one aspect of problem solving, while others misunderstand another. Some students may need help setting up equations whereas others require a better understanding of the principles involved. The computer individualizes in such cases by providing feedback and remediation tailored to the specific area of misunderstanding.

Enrichment is another way in which CAI can individualize instruction. When instructors follow a prescribed curriculum, they usually have little or no time to enrich the program for more advanced learners. CAI lessons can provide a needed supplement.

A less frequent goal for learners is observing some physical phenomenon, participating in an event, or stepping through a procedure. Some physical phenomena cannot be observed; others require more time than can be reasonably devoted within the constraints of a course. In still other instances, direct participation by a novice might endanger the life of the learner or of others. Since it is not feasible for the student to achieve the goal by direct participation, she can experience the event through the computer's simulation.

Suppose the goal is for veterinary students to become proficient in clinical diagnosis. The computer lesson enables the student to simulate the real life experience without causing needless harm to sick animals. The student asks questions about an animal and the computer responds with appropriate information. When the student decides that he has enough information, he makes a diagnosis and recommends a treatment. The computer tells him whether the diagnosis is correct and whether the treatment would help the animal get well. The computer can also tell him why his treatment is not the best and what questions he should have asked, but did not. In this case the computer simulation enables the student to sharpen his cognitive and diagnostic skills by providing the opportunity to formulate questions and interpret results.

The computer can allow the student to observe natural phenomena and manipulate parameters. For example, if the moon is visible in the sky, the student can learn to estimate the time of rising and setting of the moon. The CAI lesson lets the student set the phase of the moon (for example, full, crescent) and then simulates the relative motion of the sun and the moon in the sky under the chosen condition. The times of the moon's rising and setting are displayed on the screen, enabling the learner to fill in a table of data and discover the relationship between the phase and the times.

Sometimes students need to practice a particular skill, but such practice involves accompanying though unneeded practice in other skills. A unique role for CAI is to allow students to practice the deficient skill while removing unneeded practice in the others. For example, students in an introductory course in graphic design are required to choose a set of aesthetic values and then create a design that exemplifies those values. In traditional instruction, students expend considerable effort creating the design. They often find that it is not consistent with the aesthetic value they have chosen and they usually don't want to spend the time needed to alter their work. Rather than redo their design they change their aesthetic values to fit the one they have already created. A CAI lesson has been developed that enables the student to generate the design on the computer and to alter it with a minimum of effort. Thus the student can maintain his original aesthetic values and change his design to conform. Moreover, the lesson has an additional benefit. Since all designs are created on the computer, they all have the same technical quality. Instructors' evaluations of the designs are therefore based only on the design and not on the students' manual skills.

CAI lessons may enable an instructor to rearrange an entire course, providing greater overall benefits to the students. A foreign-language instructor may wish to spend more class time discussing the foreign country's culture, but is unable to do so because, traditionally, so much class time is spent on vocabulary or grammar drills. The instructor designs CAI lessons for those drills and thus frees class time for more discussions and cultural content. The role of the computer in this case is to help students with memorization tasks.

The goal(s) need not be limited to instructing one person at a time. Most CAI lessons are written for learners to study independently, but lessons can also be generated to incorporate student interaction with each other. CAI lessons have been used effectively with elementary-school children to promote interaction between them, to motivate, and to improve skills.

Adult learners also like to interact with others, at least some of the time. In a pilot project, three American universities developed a (non-CAI) curriculum in which students did not have to be on campus but could study at home and meet with other students and course tutors, on a voluntary basis, at study centers. Evaluation of the program revealed that students were spending about 25% of the total course time at the study center. They did not want to study alone, and interaction with other students was very important to them.

CAI lessons for more than one person frequently take the form of challenging games, which can promote cooperation or competition. A lesson may be a vehicle for students to work together to solve problems and make decisions, as in a simulation of managing a presidential campaign.

Role of the lesson in the curriculum.   If a CAI lesson is to be used, it must fit in the curriculum; the author should specify the intended use of the lesson. CAI may be the only medium of instruction for certain parts of a course. If some topics in a course are very complex and others relatively straightforward, the instructor may wish to discuss the complex ones extensively. Since there is not enough time to discuss the other topics in the classroom, those topics are taught entirely via CAI. Sometimes an institution does not have adequate faculty to teach all of the students who signed up for a course, say, programming in BASIC. A solution is to transfer part of the instructional load to the computer. Rather than teach all of the topics to half of the students, the instructors teach half of the topics to all of the students; the other half of the topics are taught via CAI. Perhaps a science curriculum includes a section on genetics, but the school does not have laboratory facilities to study genetics. A CAI lesson simulates the laboratory experience.

The CAI lesson may be one of many media used to teach a particular topic. The lesson may be an introduction to a topic, to be followed by a class discussion. In another role, it may follow classroom instruction, to review principles, apply concepts, or perfect a skill. The lesson may serve an intermediate purpose between introductory and concluding aspects of instruction. For instance, after a lecture about how to find a fault in an electrical system, the learner practices the fault-finding strategy in the CAI lesson and then finds faults in a real system.

Guidelines for Writing Goals

State the goals as precisely and clearly as possible. Say exactly what the learner will do, not what the lesson will teach or what the student will learn about. Tell the learners that they will solve velocity problems, rather than say the lesson is about velocity. State that "The learner will punctuate compound sentences" rather than "The lesson is about punctuation."

Think of the role of the CAI lesson in the course to add precision to the goals. If the lesson supplements instruction presented in the classroom, specify what the learner will accomplish in this supplement. Will the learner apply some rules learned in the classroom, such as changing the tense of verbs from present to future? If the CAI lesson is a review, what are the learners supposed to accomplish in the review? Will they memorize the meanings of some musical terms, perfect a skill learned elsewhere, or bring an ability to a specified standard of performance? If the skill is arithmetic computation initially learned in the classroom, the goal of the CAI lesson may be to attain a certain speed, say, to solve each problem within five seconds. If the role of the lesson is preparation for a subsequent task, such as a chemistry experiment, think of what aspect of the experiment the lesson is preparing students to do. The goal of the CAI lesson may be "to correctly assemble the apparatus for the experiment."

Some goals are not easily expressed by a statement of a single activity, such as solving problems. Suppose the purpose of the lesson is to understand sexual reproduction in plants. What is meant by *understand*? In this case, the best way to be specific is to generate a few sample questions that would indicate understanding. "What are the steps in the reproductive cycle?" or "What is the role of insects in pollination?" You will be able to write a complete set of such questions at a later point in lesson development (after the task analysis).

Above all, avoid the tendency to express goals ambiguously: "to provide experience." If you define the goals this vaguely, you are making the implicit assumption that the learners will understand what they should learn from this experience and know which observations to make, which questions to ask, and which conclusions to draw. Such an assumption is not valid. There is no way of predicting what novice students will learn from the experience, if anything. The situation is much like taking a class to a museum. A trip can be very enriching; however, if you do not define the goals more precisely, some students will not learn anything from the trip. They will merely go through the museum looking, but not absorbing anything. This is not to say that experiences are not worthwhile, but rather, that it is difficult to ascertain their learning value. There is a significant difference between a lesson that allows a learner to simulate an experience and a lesson that also guides her toward learning something specific. All you can say about the former is that the lesson provides students with the opportunity for self-instruction. However, the lesson itself offers no instruction.

When planning a simulation or other technique you have not tried before, generate some tentative goals. Think of some prototype questions the learner should be able to answer after doing the lesson. Suppose the topic of instruction is statistical sampling theory, and you want the students to gain insights about how the theory works in practice. Since it is not practical for the students to carry out actual surveys, you write a CAI lesson to simulate survey sampling. How can goals be stated for this simulation?

One possibility: "To compare the precision of the results of two surveys which have different numbers of respondents." Another goal, "To compare the relative precision of surveys that are based on two different sampling designs" (for example, random and stratified).

Task Analysis

The next step, after characterizing the target population and stating the lesson goals, is determining what the students have to learn to achieve those goals. To do so, analyze the task.

It may seem to be just common sense to propose that you must know what the students are supposed to learn before you can prepare instruction. True, but it is stated here for two reasons: (1) to emphasize that it is the first step, and (2) because the content is not the only aspect of the task that must be analyzed. Learning strategies for accomplishing the task, appropriate organization of the content, and analysis of novice learners' misconceptions are also part of the task analysis.

Content.   First there is the obvious analysis, the knowledge base of the task; that is, its specific body of principles, rules, definitions, and concepts. If the task is to learn the addition facts, the knowledge base includes counting ordered sets of numbers and combining sets. If the task is diagnosing a disease of the eye, the knowledge base includes the anatomy of the eye and its circulatory system.

Learning strategies.   There is far more to the task analysis than the content alone; students need procedures and strategies to accomplish the task. Some students know what to do but not how to do it; they know they should scan a list but don't know how to start. Some students simply do not know how to learn; others know strategies but do not know when it is appropriate to apply them. If the goal is to learn the addition facts, analysis of the content indicates that the learner must know how to add two numbers by counting the objects in a combined set. The content analysis does not tell the student how to remember the facts without going through the manipulation of combining sets for each fact (to add 9 + 3, count the 9 objects and then continue counting the set of 3 objects). Most students generate some system for remembering the sums but others do not. The latter understand the concept of addition but lack a learning strategy, so they need instruction in how to remember.

Sometimes immature learners don't know that they can generate a useful strategy by applying available skills. Given the task of memorizing a long list, for example, experienced learners know that organizing the words by categories makes the task easier. While ten-year-old children are capable of categorizing words, they do not spontaneously employ this skill when asked to memorize such a list. Rather, they rehearse the list; that is, they say the words over and over. The lesson designer need merely show them how to use their skills to accomplish the task more easily.

Organization of content.   Another consideration in the task analysis is the organization of the content. Though knowledge can be organized in many ways, one organization may be more useful than another for a given goal. Some learners, particularly novices in a subject, remember knowledge in the way it is presented during instruction. In subsequent tasks they find it difficult to draw on this knowledge because they cannot reorganize it in a way that is useful for this new task.

For example, in medicine, knowledge about the human body can be organized by subject such as anatomy, physiology, or the circulatory system. Alternatively, this information can be organized by organs of the body such as the heart, thus bringing together from anatomy, physiology, and other areas everything related to the heart. Information about contagious diseases can be studied by disease, grouping all information about a single disease, such as causes, symptoms, and treatment of measles. An alternative organization is by symptoms, putting together a list of all diseases that produce a fever and a rash, such as measles and scarlet fever. When diagnosing a patient who has a fever and a rash, a doctor is more likely to draw on the latter organization of knowledge than on the former. All of these examples demonstrate that there is frequently more than one way to organize knowledge, hence instruction. The decision on how to organize it should be guided by your goals for the learner.

Novices' difficulties.   Authors who have taught the content of the lessson to the target population on a one-to-one basis should recall and list the concepts, rules, and strategies that the learners find most difficult. Analyze the reasons for the difficulties. Perhaps the learners confuse two similar rules. Perhaps they use incorrect rules that just happen to lead to the right answer part of the time. If you can anticipate what learners will fail to learn or what they will learn incorrectly, you can generate instruction to minimize the chances that such errors in learning will occur.

Sometimes students, particularly children, think that using a particular strategy is cheating. For example, they are accustomed to problem solving in their heads. Consequently, if a complex reasoning problem involves remembering a considerable amount of information, they find it difficult because they try to keep track of all that information in their heads. They can, but don't, invoke the strategy of using a memory aid, such as writing down the information. Awareness of such learning problems enables the lesson author to suggest these strategies to the learners as part of the instruction.

No unique analysis.   There is no such thing as a unique task analysis. Another knowledgeable person might do the analysis in a way quite different from yours. Neither of you is necessarily right or wrong. In fact, after designing and testing the instruction, you may want to revise your own task analysis.

Alphabetizing a list of words will serve as an example of a task that can be analyzed in many ways. Before reading on, write a list of eight or ten words and alphabetize them. Then analyze the procedures you used to accomplish the task. What was the first step? How did you decide what to do next? What decisions were necessary? Were any special learning strategies employed (for example, mnemonic devices for remembering)? How did you know when to quit?

Three different strategies for alphabetizing are presented here. The first is to scan the entire list from beginning to end, for words that start with the letter *a*. Write them in a separate list and cross them off in the given one. Do the same for *b* and all succeeding letters until the list is exhausted. Then repeat the procedure for the second letter of words starting with *a*; repeat again for third and succeeding letters until no two words have the same beginning letters. Repeat the procedure for words starting with *b* or the succeeding letters in the alphabet until the list is exhausted.

A different way of alphabetizing is by "bubbling" to the top. In this system, compare the initial letters of successive pairs of words, and move up the one with the earlier letter. Suppose the first six words of a list are:

horse
animal
bear
zebra
alligator
elephant

Compare *horse* and *animal*. *A* comes before *h,* so move *animal* above *horse*:

animal
horse
bear
zebra
alligator
elephant

Compare *bear* and *horse*. *B* comes before *h,* so move *bear* before *horse*. Compare *bear* and *animal*. *B* comes after *a*, so go on to the next pair.

animal
bear
horse
zebra
alligator
elephant

A third strategy is to divide the words into two groups, those beginning with *a–m* and those with *n–z*. Continue to subdivide into smaller and smaller groups.

Although the primary purpose of this activity was to demonstrate that even a simple task can be accomplished in more than one way, an additional point was intended. Some tasks may be hard to analyze because you do them so readily that you don't have to think about how to do them. However, for the novice learner, the mere statement of a rule may be insufficient instruction. The learner may know what the words in the rules say, but not know how to do what they say. An important part of the author's task is to write instruction that helps the student learn how to learn.

The end product of the task analysis is a list of topics of instruction. This list should contain rules and definitions, relationships between topics, and procedural skills. Such skills might include directions on how to start the task and decisions about which particular strategy to invoke. The exact list of topics varies with the task and the goals of the lesson. Not all tasks, for example, require decision making.

A general procedure for task analysis is presented next. It is a prototype, which the author should adapt and modify according to the target population, goals, and content of the lesson.

Task Analysis — Procedure

A. Generate a prototype item, or more than one if the goal is stated as more than one task.
B. Do the task yourself. Write down your work as a succession of numbered steps. Show all of your work.
C. Review each of the steps, beginning with the first. On another sheet of paper, for each step, write the step number, the subject matter knowledge, and the skills or strategies you employed. Knowledge includes facts, rules, principles, and definitions. Skills include processes, decisions that were made (how to start), and criteria for making them.
D. Summarize the analysis of knowledge and skills that you have just completed into a list of topics.

An abbreviated illustration of this procedure follows. (A complete task analysis is exemplified by the sample lesson on engineering calculations, at the completion of the entire discussion of initial planning.)

Assume the goal is to organize a given body of information into outline form for term papers and the target population is high-school juniors.

A. Generate a prototype task. Organize information relating to school cafeteria:

gristly hamburger
long lines
greasy French fries
no pizza
not enough places to sit
milk costs too much

B. Do the task and write down your work. The first three steps are as follows:

1. gristly hamburger
2.   long lines
3. greasy French fries

C. Review each step to determine the knowledge and processes applied.

1. Check the entire list to get an overview of the kinds of information given. On another piece of paper, write down the first item in the list, gristly hamburger.
2. Read the next item in the list, long lines. Is it related to the first item? No. The first item has to do with food, the second with convenience. Write the second item in another column.
3. Read the next item in the list, greasy French fries. Is it related to the first item? Yes. Write it in the same column.

D. Summarize the knowledge and skills. Examples of two topics are:

1. Scan the list for facts that are related.
2. Generate unifying themes for these relationships.

Detailed Analysis

After generating the list of topics, the author will need to ascertain how much additional instruction to provide for each. Knowledge can be analyzed into successively simpler subtopics and components down to the most elementary concepts, such as the sounds of the letters of the alphabet. Obviously, all prerequisite knowledge will not be taught in the lesson. The author must establish an entry point, knowledge that is specifically prerequisite to the particular lesson.

The sequence of topics, must be arranged. When you as expert accomplished the task, you drew on knowledge and skills in a given sequence. That sequence may be different from the order in which the knowledge should be presented to novice learners.

A detailed task analysis enables the author to specify prerequisite skills and to decide how to organize the knowledge for instructional presentation. In addition, the detailed analysis provides a basis for generating specific goals later when you develop the units of instruction.

Review the summary list of topics that was generated by the task analysis. For each topic, decide whether the target students will have the prerequisite knowledge. If not, analyze the topic further, the way you did the initial gross analysis. Stop the analysis at the point where you expect the learners to have the required knowledge. Define the latter as prerequisite skills. Identify the skills that must be taught for sure and those the student might be able to learn simultaneously with essential instruction. It may not be necessary to design instruction for every single step to achieve learning. Plan to design instruction, at first, for just those steps that are major. Later on, testing the instruction with students will provide a basis for deciding which topics should be added to the main line of instruction and which can either be included as extra help for students who need it or be excluded altogether.

Prerequisite Skills

Prerequisite skills are defined as the skills and knowledge the student needs specifically for a task. These skills emerge as a consequence of detailed task analysis.

It cannot be assumed that all members of the target population already have the prerequisite skills. For example, suppose the goal of the lesson is to organize a body of information in outline form. If the target population is high-school juniors, you can anticipate a minimum reading level for most students. However, it cannot be assumed that most high-school juniors have acquired the prerequisite skill, knowing the structure of an outline.

In CAI, a short pretest can be presented at the beginning of a lesson to determine whether the student has the prerequisite knowledge. If the student lacks the prerequisite, the lesson can recommend resources for making up this deficiency. Alternatively, brief reviews can be added to the lesson for students who need a little refresher.

Evaluation Measures

An important aspect of developing a lesson is evaluating it to determine if learners have achieved the specified goals. Although the actual evaluation of students' performance takes place at a later time in lesson development, measures should be planned and generated as much as possible at this time.

You may be able to generate all of the evaluation measures during initial planning for the overall lesson, particularly if you have taught the subject matter before. Questions may be taken from a set already available in your files. However, in developing instruction in this subject matter for the first time, you may be prepared to develop only sample or prototype questions at this point. For example, you may know the kinds of questions to ask but not the exact content. If the lesson involves a novel approach, it may be difficult to specify exactly how to evaluate performance. Nevertheless, plan some specific, though tentative, measures and describe them as accurately as possible. Later, after developing and evaluating the units of instruction, you can revise and improve your evaluation measures.

For some goals, performance can be evaluated by the same kinds of items suitable for other media, such as traditional types of questions, including open-ended, multiple-choice, matching, and so on. Such questions may be suitable if your goal is the acquisition of knowledge or the application of rules. *Write the specific evaluation questions now, to be given at the end of the lesson.*

Reaching the goal of the CAI lesson may itself be the evaluation measure. An example is a lesson in which the goal is to get tenure in a teaching job. The lesson simulates the situations encountered by beginning teachers. The learner interacts with different people who can affect the chances of getting tenure: the principal, students, other faculty, and parents. In one situation, for example, the learner (beginning teacher) must decide whether to submit to pressure from the department head to join the union; in another, whether to report students' breaches of school discipline to the principal. Success or failure in getting tenure at the end of the lesson is the measure of the student teacher's performance.

In some lessons the goal is to show a specific level of skill while stepping through a process. In that case the measures will be neither posttest items nor completion of the lesson, but some other indication of proficiency. It might be the time taken or the average number of tries required to perform correctly. If the goal is to find the faulty component in an electrical system, the measure could be the time needed to find the fault or the proportion of tests made that resulted in useful information.

At this point, *plan evaluation measures* of student performance to the extent that it is possible to do so. Remember that the measures can be revised and/or completed after further development of the lesson.

SAMPLE LESSON

A sample lesson will now be generated to illustrate initial planning at the lesson level. Although the subject matter of this example is engineering calculations, no knowledge about engineering is needed to understand the presentation.

Background

This lesson was developed in response to a need perceived by an instructor. A short history is presented here to provide an understanding of how this lesson evolved. College students take engineering courses in which an important component is making engineering calculations. Solving these problems requires skill in manipulating quantities with units of measure (for example, converting 55 miles per hour to feet per second). The students have already worked with problems involving units in prerequisite courses. Although instructors stress the importance of units, students solve problems by substituting numbers for symbols, but treat the units as an incidental part of the problem, to be tacked on after the numerical computation is completed. Engineering problems do not always have prescribed formulas, so strategies that students have previously employed may no longer be applicable. The key to solving engineering problems is manipulating the units. In class the professor does discuss strategies for doing engineering calculations with units, but course time is so limited that he can spend only a short time on this topic. Many students need more time to go over the procedures themselves in order to become proficient at doing such calculations. The goal is to calculate quickly, as well as correctly.

Target Population

The target population is average-ability sophomore-level college students majoring in engineering.

Goal

The purpose of the lesson is to review the strategies for doing engineering calculations (previously taught in class) and to practice doing such calculations efficiently and correctly. A tutoring staff is unavailable, so CAI is chosen to provide the guided practice.

Task Analysis

What does a student have to know in order to do engineering calculations?
  A. Begin the task analysis by picking a prototype problem. A nontechnical version of a prototype problem is presented here:
     Gasoline costs 32.7 cents per liter. What is the dollar cost of 5 gallons of gas?

B. Do the task. Solve the problem and keep a record of the work.

1. $= ?$ dollars

2. $\dfrac{32.7 \text{ cents}}{\text{liter}}$ $= ?$ dollars

3. $\dfrac{32.7 \text{ cents}}{\text{liter}} \times 5 \text{ gal.}$ $= ?$ dollars

4. 3.8 liters $= 1$ gallon;   100 cents $= 1$ dollar

5. $\dfrac{3.8 \text{ liters}}{1 \text{ gallon}} = 1$ $\dfrac{1 \text{ dollar}}{100 \text{ cents}} = 1$

6. $\dfrac{32.7 \text{ cents}}{\text{liter}} \times 5 \text{ gal.} \times \dfrac{3.8 \text{ liters}}{1 \text{ gal.}} \times \dfrac{1 \text{ dollar}}{100 \text{ cents}} = ?$ dollars

7. $\dfrac{32.7 \text{ cents}}{\text{liter}} \times 5 \text{ gal.} \times \dfrac{3.8 \text{ liters}}{1 \text{ gal.}} \times \dfrac{1 \text{ dollar}}{100 \text{ cents}} = \$6.21$

C. Review each step and record the knowledge and skills applied.
   1. Read the problem, and look for the units asked for in the answer. It is dollars. Write "? dollars" on the right side of the paper and put " $=$ " in front.
   2. Prepare to write the rest of the information given in the problem on the left side of the " $=$." Since the unit asked for in the answer is money, write the quantity involving the money unit in the numerator; write it in mathematical notation in order to be able to perform mathematical operations later.
   3. Multiply by 5 gallons, so that both the numerator and denominator will have measures of volume.
   4. The objective is to cancel the units of volume on the left so that the units in the result will be money; the unit of money needed is dollars, the same as on the right side of the equation. It is impossible to cancel units because the equation has two different measures of volume, liters and gallons. Furthermore, the left side of the equation shows cents and the answer must be in dollars. It is necessary to convert one set of units to another. To do so, use the equivalence relationships between the measures.
   5. Use algebra to convert each equivalence equation to a ratio equal to 1.
   6. Multiply the left side of the equation by the ratios that are equal to 1.
   7. Do the multiplication and division, first with units and then with numbers. Notice that all the units (liters, gallons, and cents) cancel, leaving the desired units, dollars, in the answer.

D. Finally, review the protocols and summarize the knowledge and processes required to do the task. In this example, the two aspects are summarized separately.

Knowledge required:

1. How to write units in mathematical notation.
2. How to use identities (for example, 3.8 liters = 1 gallon) to convert one set of units to another.
3. How to do arithmetic operations with units.

Strategies and procedures:

1. The key is knowing how to start.
2. Knowing how to use the rest of the information given in the problem.
3. Knowing where to get the information about equivalent measures.
4. Knowing how to decide which ratios to use, such as 3.8 liters/gal or 1 gal/3.8 liters.

A word of caution is in order here. It is not necessary to attempt to operationalize the distinctions between "knowledge" and "strategies and processes," or to devote an excessive amount of time deciding how to categorize each step in the task. The two categories are presented to emphasize the point that the analysis must include more than content; it must analyze the learning strategies and techniques, the knowing how and why and what.

Since the author of the engineering lesson had previous experience teaching this content on a one-to-one basis, he had noted a particular error that many students made: They began the problem by writing down the numerical values given and ignored the units until after they computed the answer. The CAI lesson should try to prevent this error.

Even though you may disagree with this analysis in part or in its entirety, remember that there is no such thing as a unique task analysis. Consider this one for the sake of expediency. The next step is a more detailed analysis of each topic.

Detailed Analysis

Recall that the purpose of the detailed analysis is to determine prerequisite skills, organize the content of the lesson, and provide a basis for generating subgoals for each of the units of instruction.

The first topic is using mathematical notation for units. To do so, identify the units part of the measured quantities. This step requires the knowledge that measured quantities are described by both number and unit (for example, 3 feet), which in turn requires an understanding of the concept of measurement. The target population has this knowledge, so note that understanding the concept of measurement is a prerequisite.

Next topic, identities. Convert quantities from one set of units to another by multiplying by conversion factors. This multiplication is possible because each of the conversion factors is equal to one, and multiplying by one does not change the value of an expression. Generate the conversion factors by starting with identities. Some are equivalent relationships in a single measurement system, for example, both cents and dollars. Other identities relate units within one measuring system to another, such as metric to English system (3.8 liters = 1 gallon). Using algebra, rewrite each identity as a ratio equal to 1. In fact, it is possible to generate two conversion ratios from each identity, each equal to 1, 3.8 liters/gallon and 1 gallon/3.8 liters. The target students know how to do the algebra, so the analysis is complete at this point. Note that the ability to do algebraic manipulations is a prerequisite.

Next topic, arithmetic operations. Here units must be expressed in mathematical symbols (for example, ft. × ft. or ft.² rather than square feet). In symbolic notation, multiply and divide units as in arithmetic. Assume that the target population can multiply and divide fractions, so analyze no further and list this skill as a prerequisite.

The strategies are also analyzed in greater detail. For example, to solve the problem, read it to see what units it asked for in the answer. Write down that part of the answer and a "?" for the numerical part to indicate that it is not yet known.

There are two sources of information for solving the problem: (1) information given in the problem and (2) information about equivalence relationships (identities) in measurement, taken from personal knowledge, but also available in handbooks.

Since it is possible to generate two ratios equal to one from each identity (1 gallon/3.8 liters and 3.8 liters/1 gallon) decide which one to choose. Pick the one that enables you to cancel out the units you do not want in the answer and leaves the units you do want.

Recall some of the difficulties learners exhibited when doing these problems. A major problem was that in working with measured quantities they were accustomed to manipulating the numerical part and tacking on the units at the end. For all practical purposes they ignored the units. Instruction should, therefore, emphasize the units.

After completing the detailed analyses, the organization and the sequence of topics are planned. Since the learner needs the basic knowledge about units and conversion factors as tools for solving the problems, those concepts will be presented first, before problem-solving strategies. To sequence the "knowledge" topics, it is evident that in order to manipulate identities, a student has to know how to manipulate units. Therefore, the first topic will be mathematical notation and the next, arithmetic operations with units, followed by identities and their application as conversion ratios. Succeeding topics will be strategies for writing the equations sequenced in the order stated.

Evaluation Measures

Problems from the engineering professor's files are examined. Those that are consistent with the goals of the lesson are retained. Additional problems will be generated if the available set proves to be inadequate. The CAI lesson will be evaluated by a conventional paper-and-pencil test.

Thus, the introductory planning has been completed. The next step is the creation of the instructional units.

RIPPLE PLAN: UNIT LEVEL

Up to this point we have discussed the initial components at the overall lesson level. Now we focus on the second phase, producing instruction at the unit level.

Rationale

Developing instructional units involves actually producing the lesson on the computer, in addition to planning and creating it on paper. Since the lesson is CAI, creation entails much more than just writing the text. Creation includes planning interaction: posing questions, judging responses, and commenting on those responses. Equally important is the planning for smooth human-machine interaction and for managing the instruction.

In CAI, it is not practical to make the plans and decisions for every component of instruction before writing the computer program. An author may wish to develop and test only part of a lesson before making final decisions about how to present it, particularly if the lesson is innovative. The computer enables her to do so.

There is no need to make extensive plans and expend considerable time programming an entire lesson only to discover later that the instructional design is faulty. The author can avoid this pitfall by interacting with others as each unit is produced. Experience has shown that authors are less reluctant to incorporate comments and suggestions of colleagues if only part, rather than the entire lesson, requires revision.

Components

The recommendation to generate one part of the lesson at a time is not a recommendation to program at the terminal with no planning beyond the initial phase. A systematic and efficient procedure is required. Such a procedure is the function of the Ripple Plan (Fig. 2.3). The plan has two parts, the band of concentric circles and the box. The circles represent the planning, creation, and revision of materials off-line, not on the computer. Each circle is one component of unit development: Presentation, Responses and Feedback, and Human Factors and Management. The box represents the implementation and evaluation of those plans: programming the computer to produce the actual product, and testing it. The basic idea is to plan, program, and evaluate one component before expanding the unit to include additional components.

Procedure

Start at the inside circle, with the presentation. Plan the presentation: write the script and prepare the diagrams, as well as the questions and exercises. After completing this aspect, leave this circle to produce the presentation by

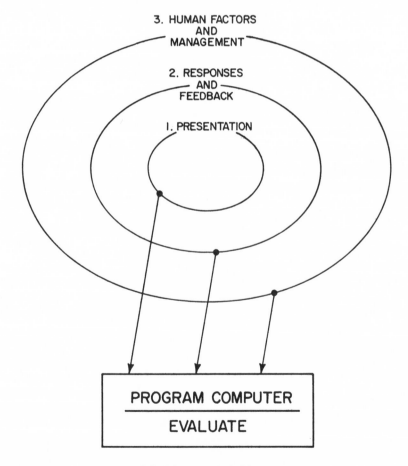

FIG. 2.3   The Ripple Plan.

writing the computer program. Next, evaluate the program by doing it yourself as a student, as well as by asking a colleague or some students to do so. Use this tryout to gather information on how to improve the presentation. You may find, for instance, that too much information appears on a given display at one time, or perhaps an explanation is not clearly presented. During this test, notice whether students give answers you had not anticipated, either right ones or wrong.

On completion of tryout, return to the next circle in the Ripple Plan: Responses and Feedback. Based on the evaluation you have just completed, plan revisions to the presentation. Add to the list of acceptable correct responses those that you had not anticipated but that are correct. Generate feedback for incorrect responses you had not anticipated. Decide how to help students who had difficulty understanding the instruction. Again, leave the circles to program and evaluate. Try out the lesson and get others to do so, too. Notice whether your revisions improved the lesson and what further revisions might be needed.

On completion of this tryout, return to the next circle: Management and Human Factors decisions. Decide such matters as the conditions under which the student is allowed to advance in the instruction, and whether to allow the student to ask for help or to provide it automatically. Try to achieve smooth student-machine interaction; for example, show the learner how to enter special characters, like scientific symbols or superscripts.

Some decisions that you make may be relevant only to this particular topic of instruction; others will affect the entire lesson. For example, you may decide to set a criterion of performance in the unit, perhaps that 75% of the exercises must be done correctly on the first try. You may possibly use this management rule throughout the lesson or choose it for this topic only.

Make revisions as shown necessary by the previous testing. Again, program, evaluate, and revise.

Note that the purpose of evaluation is different during implementation of the Ripple Plan than during initial planning of the overall lesson. In the Ripple Plan you are evaluating the lesson itself. Here, the goals of evaluation are to make the instruction as effective as possible and communication with the computer as smooth as possible. To accomplish this, monitor students' ongoing performance.

In the next three chapters we consider how to implement each of the three circles in the Ripple Plan (Presentation, Responses and Feedback, and Human factors/Management) and the accompanying box (Program and Evaluate). Further development of our sample lesson on engineering calculations continues to illustrate the process.

After the units of instruction are finished, focus returns to the overall lesson. The components of lesson completion, the third phase, are introduced here, and discussed fully in chapters 6 and 7.

OVERVIEW OF COMPLETION: LESSON LEVEL

Management and Human Factors

In generating the lesson, human factors and management decisions are made for the individual units. At the lesson level, plans are made for managing the flow of instruction between units and for uniformly smooth human-machine interaction. For example, you should communicate to the learners what the computer will expect of them and what they can expect from the computer. If students must enter special characters, like super-scripts, the computer must teach them how to do so and also inform them that information about these special keys is always available. Decide also who will manage the learners' path of instruction through the lesson: the computer, the learner, the classroom instructor, or some combination of these. For those aspects of instruction under computer control, plan rules for advancing through the lesson.

Introductory Displays

Every lesson must have a title page. Most lessons have an index or table of contents or "menu." Other introductory displays include one or more of the following: an explanation of the function and use of special-purpose keys, the purpose of the lesson, and special information or rules if the lesson is a game or simulation.

Concluding Displays

Learners have to be told that the lesson has ended and, when it has, what options are available to them. Perhaps they can access an index to review selected sections of the lesson; perhaps you merely want them to leave the lesson or even to start again from the beginning. In any case, they have no way of knowing what they can do next unless you inform them.

Evaluation and Revision

You don't know if the lesson as a whole has accomplished its goals until students from the target population have tried it. These trials enable you to evaluate the lesson and revise it.

Documentation

The documentation provides decision-making information to potential users of the lesson(s). It should include the topics covered in the lesson, the goals, prerequisites, target population, instructional techniques used, special features, number of students who tested the completed lesson, and results of student trials.

Before we discuss developing the lesson at the instructional unit level, let us consider the pros and cons of learning to do your own programming.

SHOULD THE LESSON AUTHOR LEARN HOW TO PROGRAM?

A CAI lesson must be programmed for the computer. You will have to decide whether to learn the language of your CAI system well enough to do all of your own programming or to have another person do that programming. Whether you choose the former or the latter, it is important that you achieve at least a minimal acquaintance with the programming language. To be effective as a lesson author, you must understand the capabilities and limitations of the CAI system. The best way to do so is to learn the basic elements and do some simple programming yourself. As the lesson author, you also need a basis of communication with the programmer. Lesson designers who have no knowledge of the programming language have been known to ask programmers to make changes in a program that add little to its effectiveness but add hours of work revising the program. Sometimes designers who know nothing about programming keep changing their minds about how they want the lessson to go. The result is an unfortunate cycle: The programmer prepares a unit of work and then the designer decides to do the lesson differently. Programmers find it frustrating to discard large segments of work even though they are paid to do it. To understand their point of view, you must have the experience yourself of programming a lesson, however short or simple.

This is not to suggest that you must do all of your own programming. Working with a programmer does have distinct advantages; you can devote most of your time to lesson design and leave the intricacies of the programming to the specialist. If you have no previous experience and see no need to become a proficient programmer, this group approach is certainly more efficient. This efficiency does not happen automatically, however; you must lay some groundwork for smooth operation of the group. To work successfully with the programmer, preplan and consider each section of the lesson carefully before you give it to him or her. Program a few of the displays to see how you like them before assigning the work to the programmer. A display does not always produce the same effect on the screen as on paper. After it is on the screen you will know what needs changing. It is impossible to avoid programming revisions completely; it is possible to keep them to a minimum.

Another reason for preparing some preliminary displays or program segments is that the task will enable you to provide the programmer with a more precise understanding of what you are trying to accomplish. Few programmers have training in education. They often get carried away with all of the clever things they can get the CAI system to do. As a result, the lesson they create may be quite different from the one you intended. Your preliminary efforts in designing prototypic displays will minimize misunderstandings and preclude unnecessary programmer pyrotechnics.

If you choose to learn the language and do all of your own programming, you will progress more rapidly if you avoid the two most common pitfalls of beginners: (1) trying to learn the entire language before writing any segment of a lesson and (2) shortcutting by copying, without understanding, programs written by others. Some beginners do find it useful to learn by using other authors' programs as models. This method of learning is effective only if you understand the logical basis of the program. If you copy without understanding, you will lack the knowledge needed to make adaptations of the model for other programs you wish to implement. You will spend hours of time later "debugging" your lesson (trying to figure out why your revisions or adaptations of the model cause errors in the program). The other extreme, trying to learn the entire language at once, is also impractical. Since only a small portion of the programming language is needed for each application, learn whatever portion you need at the time. Experiment with the features you have used to see what additional effects can be generated with them. With each new application, learn the additional features needed.

If at all possible, obtain the consulting services of an experienced programmer when starting out. The usual advice for debugging (finding errors in) a program is, "Write a trial segment of code (program) and test it out to track down the problem." That advice is fine if you are knowledgeable enough to make hypotheses about the potential sources of the error. As a beginner, you are not likely to have this knowledge and may find it very frustrating and time-consuming to try to locate the error yourself. An expert can quickly help you over the troublesome spot by detecting the source of the difficulty immediately and prescribing a solution, or by demonstrating the "try it and see what happens" procedure.

3 Ripple Plan: Presentation

INTRODUCTION

You are now at the start of the Ripple Plan, the innermost circle, ready to create the presentation: the text, the related diagrams, and the questions. Technical aspects of the presentation, such as display designing and attention-getting techniques, are discussed in chapter 6.

Clarity

It is impossible to overemphasize the importance of clear and careful instructional presentation in CAI. In the classroom, an instructor is available to answer questions and to restate information if it is poorly or inadequately presented. In CAI a human being will not necessarily be there to answer questions when students are studying the lesson. Even if an instructor is present, it is not likely to be the author. If the lesson is not clear, neither the instructor nor the students will be able to understand it, and the lesson will be of little value. The anecdote is told that when Robert Browning was courting Elizabeth Barrett she asked him to explain one of the poems he had written, which she did not understand. He replied that when he wrote the poem, only he and God understood it. Now God alone understood it. Don't let your CAI lessons suffer the same fate.

System Compatibility

The author's primary goal in designing the instructional presentation is to make the lesson as effective as possible. Care must be exercised, however, that the design be feasible for the computer system for which the lesson is planned. Computer systems vary widely in both hardware and software capabilities, such as the size of the display screen, graphic capability, speed of display, and the programming languages. Instructional designs vary in the demands they make of the system. If the lesson requires extensive graphics, for example, the system must be capable of displaying them quickly. The lesson will lose the student's attention if the display plots too slowly. Some systems are capable of handling graphics adequately; others are not. Sometimes the author can alter the presentation by substituting one display technique for another, with no loss in effectiveness. In other instances a computer expert can help the author overcome the apparent limitations of the computer system by applying advanced programming techniques. If neither is possible, the author must choose a viable system or abandon the design for one that suits the available system. Above all, do NOT sacrifice the quality of the lesson merely to generate it for CAI. The following story illustrates the point.

Until recently, one of the popular personal microcomputer systems displayed all text in uppercase letters. Some individuals, who were producing lessons for use with this system, created a lesson in capitalization using all uppercase letters! The authors distinguished between uppercase and lowercase by using the inverse mode for capital letters. (In inverse mode the colors of the letters and the background are inverted; rather than a green character on black background, the display shows a black character on green). The lessons caused the students needless bother and confusion.

Innovative Presentations

If you are planning an innovative presentation and using a teaching technique you have never used before, do a dry run first. Write the script for the lesson and try it with some students before programming it. Play the role of the computer when testing the lesson in order to gain insight into the students' perceptions of the task and to decide whether the technique is feasible for CAI. Suppose, for example, that a lesson is contemplated in which the computer picks a chemical element and the student is supposed to determine its name by asking questions. Beginning chemistry students may not know what information they need to obtain in order to discriminate between the elements; they don't know what questions to ask. Thus, by discovering that this questioning technique is not appropriate for these students, you have saved all of the time and effort that would have gone into programming the lesson.

If the innovative lesson is a simulation and cannot be tested in such a preliminary fashion, try to write only a section of it; program that section and ask some students to try it before doing extensive programming. Students do not always react as anticipated. Lessons that appeal to individuals knowledgeable in a subject matter area sometimes do nothing for students.

Producing the instruction is presented next, with a discussion of each step in the procedure. The process is illustrated by generating a presentation for the sample lesson on engineering calculations.

STEPS IN THE PROCEDURE

1. Generate specific goals for the unit.
2. Choose the teaching technique(s).
3. Write the script (text and diagrams).
4. Generate the questions and exercises.

GENERATE SPECIFIC GOALS

During initial planning for the overall lesson you generated certain general goals for the learner. Now, at the unit level, generate specific goals for the particular unit using the detailed task analysis of the unit as a guide. Restate the content and strategies listed in the detailed task analysis as activities the learner will demonstrate. Formulate goals precisely, just as you did when generating goals for the overall lesson. Suppose the lesson goal is to use correct structure in writing programs in Pascal. Detailed analysis of the content reveals that one of the essential concepts of the structure is the program heading. You might write the goal for that concept this way, "Use correct structure to write the program heading." Similarly, use the detailed analysis to write specific goals for the entire unit.

CHOOSE THE TEACHING TECHNIQUES

The techniques you choose depend on the subject matter, the goals, and the target population. The presentation can be direct instruction or a discovery mode. The former is basically "tell and ask." In the latter the computer guides the learner to discovering the concept by asking questions that lead the student to the concept through exploration rather than telling directly. If the subject matter is relatively simple for the target group and the knowledge prerequisite for further understanding of the overall concept, direct instruction is probably best. If the target population is capable of inferring rules or concepts in the discovery mode, and you expect them to benefit from it, then plan to use it. If the goal is the application of some rules or principles, plan a set of practice exercises. Consider employing a game format to add motivation. If improving a skill is the aim, choose a drill. It is also possible to choose some combination of teaching techniques. The strategy you select may be specific only to a single unit of instruction, or it may serve for several units or even the entire lesson.

WRITE THE SCRIPT

It is clearly beyond the scope of this book to discuss the design of scripts for every level of knowledge, from discrimination learning to complex problem solving. (See the bibliography for relevant books and journal articles.) The discussion here is limited to topics that require special attention in CAI, including guidelines for the amount or extent of the presentation, techniques for using the computer to facilitate learning, ways to keep students informed, and the use of diagrams.

Minimum but Sufficient Presentation

Author's goals.   Instruction must be sufficiently complete to ensure learning, but brevity is also important. In CAI, the size of the display screen limits the amount of information that can be presented at one time. More important, if the presentation includes unnecessary information, students' time will be wasted and they may become so bored that they will just sign out of the lesson without completing it. Extraneous text consumes computer memory and processing resources. In CAI the author should try to meet the twin goals of making presentations adequate for the students to learn the material but efficient enough not to waste students' time or computer resources. Suggestions for doing so follow.

Topics.   Focus on the critical aspects of the concept or principle, and design instruction for those aspects only. Later, when testing the lesson with students, you will be able to determine where gaps exist; the lesson can be expanded at that time. If you are not judicious in the amount of instruction generated initially, you will have no way of determining during student testing which parts could have been omitted without a loss in learning.

Text.   It is important to minimize the amount of text presented on the display. Beginning authors sometimes treat the CAI lesson as if it were classroom instruction; they write the text for the CAI lesson as if they were talking to a class. Consequently, the lesson becomes lengthy because it includes friendly asides, tangential information, and endless repetition of explanations. Such a text won't do in CAI. For some unexplained reason, students do not read the display if the entire screen is filled with text. Strange, because they read books in which entire pages are filled with text. Perhaps students have different expectations from CAI.

Keep in mind that the text will be written rather than oral. After writing the script, review it to eliminate extraneous material. Delete text that does not elucidate or illuminate the subject, as well as content that is tangential rather than essential to the explanation. In other words, be concise.

Although some students may need more thorough explanations than others, do not include them for all students. Provide the basic explanation for everybody, and make additional explanations available if needed or if requested by a learner. (More about this in the next chapter.)

Examples.   The admonition to minimize the presentation at first, or to "write lean" as is sometimes said, should not be confused with the erroneous idea that "telling is teaching" or that a single example adequately illustrates a rule or a concept. Students can learn a concept from a definition alone, but they usually need examples to help them fully understand it. Many beginning CAI authors err by giving only one example; others give many examples, but they don't add to the student's understanding. A systematic choice of examples enables the author to provide minimum yet adequate instruction. Guidelines for choosing examples follow.

Pick examples so that students can recognize every instance of a concept but at the same time not err by including in their understanding items that are not part of it. Two good rules to follow are (1) choose examples that define the whole range of the concept; and (2) simultaneously present nonexamples, that is, items that are not examples.

To select examples that illustrate the full range of the concept, analyze its critical and its variable attributes. The critical attributes are those that distinguish the concept from all others. Variable attributes are characteristics that are part of the concept but not critical in distinguishing it from others.

Consider as an example the concept of a palindrome. Webster (1976) defines a palindrome as a "word, verse, or sentence (Able was I ere I saw Elba) or a number (1881) that reads the same backward or forward." The critical attribute of the palindrome is that it reads the same backward as forward. Variable attributes are the nature of the unit (letter, word, number) and the length of the palindrome. To demonstrate the whole range of the concept, pick examples of palindromes that have different units and that have different lengths. Include some words (where the letters are the unit), some numbers, and some sentences (where the words are the units). Examples should also vary in length such as 12321 and 543676345.

To help the learner discriminate between those aspects of the concept that are critical and those that are not, present example/nonexample pairs. The nonexample in each pair has the same variable attributes as the example, but not the critical. For the concept of a palindrome, the pair, 3478743 and

3478347, are an example and a nonexample, respectively. The nonexample is the same length and has the same digits as the example. The only difference is the critical one, the *order* of the digits.

Suppose the instructional designer presents only two example-nonexample pairs to teach the concept of a palindrome (Fig. 3.1). What kinds of misconceptions could arise?

Many students would probably think that *able* is a palindrome because it appears in the sentence that is a palindrome. They would be incorrect. If a sentence is a palindrome, each *word* read backward is the same as the corresponding word read forward. If a single word is a palindrome, the *letters* read the same backward as forward. In the example, the word *able* itself is not a palindrome, but the sentence in which it is found is a palindrome. A student is less likely to make the error if the author presents example/nonexample pairs of both words and sentences (Fig. 3.2).

Another possible but less likely misconception, if the only examples are those in Fig. 3.1, is that only 4-digit numbers can be palindromes. Numerical palindromes of different lengths should be included to minimize the probability of this misunderstanding.

An effective technique to facilitate understanding is simultaneously to present sets of example-nonexample pairs, in which the examples illustrate the wide range of the concept (such as words and numbers) while associated nonexamples match closely (Fig. 3.3).

Facilitate Comprehension

Attune reading level.   Keep the reading level at or below the educational level of the target population. The objective is to teach the material, not to test the student's comprehension of a complicated text. A common shortcoming of science textbooks for elementary schools is that the reading level is above the level of the students. The students find the textbooks difficult,

A palindrome is a word, chain of words, or number that reads the same backward or forward.

Example of a palindrome:	1881
Not a palindrome:	1818

Palindrome:	Able was I ere I saw Elba.
Not a palindrome:	Able was I ere he saw Elba.

Is the word "able" a palindrome? Type yes or no.

FIG. 3.1   An insufficient number of example-nonexample pairs (just these two) may lead to misconceptions about the concept, palindrome.

A palindrome is a word, chain of words, or number that reads the same backward or forward.

Palindrome:	Able was I ere I saw Elba.
Not a palindrome:	Able was I ere he saw Elba.
Palindrome:	ere
Not a palindrome:	saw

Is the word "able" a palindrome? Type yes or no.

FIG. 3.2   Example-nonexample pairs that simultaneously illustrate both single word and sentence palindromes.

not because the scientific concepts are beyond their understanding, but because the text is. Let's not make these same mistakes in CAI.

Be explicit.   Sometimes it is simply not enough to present examples and nonexamples of a concept. It may be necessary to point out specifically the presence or absence of critical features. In Fig. 3.2, for example, the following information might have been added:

> The first sentence is a palindrome because all the words read the same backward as forward. The second sentence is not a palindrome because not all the words read the same backward as forward.

> The word *ere* is a palindrome because the letters read the same backward or forward. *Saw* is not a palindrome because the letters do not read the same backward as forward.

This extended explanation serves an additional function: It tells the student which entity to consider when deciding if a verbal expression is a palindrome.

A palindrome is a word, chain of words, or number that reads the same backward or forward.

Examples of palindromes:	1881	eke
Not palindromes:	1818	eek
Examples of palindromes:	123454321	radar
Not palindromes:	123451234	radra

FIG. 3.3   Example-nonexample pairs that illustrate variable characteristics of palindromes.

Complex explanations can sometimes be simplified by presenting the in-formation in the form of a dialogue between the student and the instructor or between two students. This method is particularly suitable for young children, but adults find it helpful too. Figures 3.4a, 3.4b, and 3.4c illustrate a dialogue. This technique can be employed on computer systems that support only simple graphics like lines and circles. Elaborate drawings are not essential.

Be precise. Exhortations to "study the examples" or "look carefully" (Fig. 3.5) do not help students learn. What are they supposed to notice

FIG. 3.4a   First display in dialogue series.

FIG. 3.4b   Additional dialogue is added to display.

FIG. 3.4c Completed dialogue showing use of dialogue to simplify a presentation. (From computer-assisted instruction lesson, *Think of a Number.* Copyright © 1976 by The Board of Trustees of the University of Illinois. Reprinted by permission.)

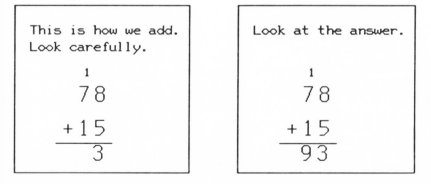

FIG. 3.5 Instruction that tells where to look, but fails to say what to look for.

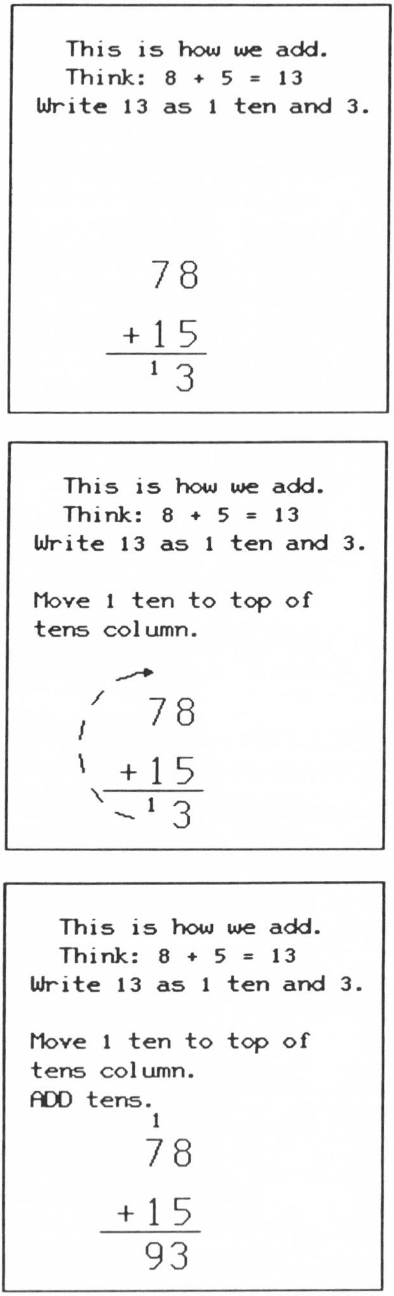

This is how we add.
Think: 8 + 5 = 13
Write 13 as 1 ten and 3.

```
  7 8
+ 1 5
¹ 3
```

This is how we add.
Think: 8 + 5 = 13
Write 13 as 1 ten and 3.

Move 1 ten to top of
tens column.

```
    7 8
  + 1 5
  ¹ 3
```

This is how we add.
Think: 8 + 5 = 13
Write 13 as 1 ten and 3.

Move 1 ten to top of
tens column.
ADD tens.

```
 1
  7 8
+ 1 5
  9 3
```

FIG. 3.6 Instruction that tells student how to think about the task as well as how to proceed.

when they do "Look at the answer" in the second display—the number 93? Now compare the instruction in Fig. 3.6 with that in Fig. 3.5. The former tells the student how to step through the process. (These figures are deliberately noninteractive here, in order to direct attention to the point that is being made and that point only.)

Tell the students precisely what they should do in order to learn rather than merely where they should look on the screen. Suppose the lesson is teaching foreign students some techniques for understanding English proverbs. Compare the presentations in Fig. 3.7a and Fig. 3.7b.

Figure 3.7a tells students to notice the underlined words, which they probably do anyhow, but not *why* the words are underlined. The precise information to be conveyed is that the words were added to make the proverb easier to understand, as in Fig. 3.7b. This precise statement provides the student with a general rule for understanding other proverbs, not merely the one on the current display.

Avoid information overload.   Students find it difficult to learn and remember a large body of information that is displayed all at once.

CARDINAL PRINCIPLE: Be judicious in the amount of material that is conveyed at one time.

If a considerable amount of text must be displayed, and it must all be shown on a single display, present only one idea or one paragraph at a time. Tell the student to press a particular key when she is ready to read on.

Another technique is to present the main topics in outline form and then explain each topic in response to the student's key presses (Figs. 3.8a and 3.8b).

If many instructions must be presented, such as rules in a game, display them one at a time and ask the student a question about each rule to be sure

---

"Better the head of a dog than the tail of a lion."
Our proverb could be worded in the following way:
It is better to be the head of a dog than the tail of a lion.
Notice the underlined words.

FIG. 3.7a   Instruction that is explicit about what to do, but not about why to do so.

"Better the head of a dog than the tail of a lion."
Add some words to make the sentence easier to understand.
It is better to be the head of a dog than the tail of a lion.

FIG. 3.7b   Instruction that states explicitly both what to do and why.

What to look for when you observe a lesson trial.

1. Programming errors:

2. Communication problems:

3. Content:

FIG. 3.8a   Outline format presents an overview of topic.

What to look for when you observe a lesson trial.

1. *Programming errors:* Execution errors, incorrect answers that are accepted as ok, correct answers that are not accepted, typographical errors.

2. Communication problems:

3. Content:

FIG. 3.8b   Text is presented for one subtopic at a time, as student requests it.

he understands it. Figure 3.9 shows all of the rules needed to play the game known as Pico-fomi. Imagine how difficult it would be for a student to remember all of this information if it were presented in this way as an entire screen full of text.

Many learners will give up and quit reading before the end of such a display. They will count on figuring out the rules later when they need to use them. Some well-motivated students will spend a considerable amount of time copying all the information onto a piece of paper.

Both of these situations can be avoided by presenting the rules one at a time (Fig. 3.10) even though doing so requires more effort: more displays, more questions, more response judging, and more computer memory. Initially, the first paragraph and the request to guess a number are displayed (Fig. 3.10a). After the learner responds correctly, the multiple-choice question is added (Fig. 3.10b). Finally, after the learner responds to the questions, the computer displays an appropriate message (Fig. 3.10c). Good instruction in CAI obviously requires effort. If the objective is for the student to develop strategies to win the game, don't make it hard for her to learn the rules. Help her learn how to play the game without confusing rules to hamper her.

Keep Students Informed

The author can help students learn by telling them what to expect, what they will be required to do, and how the instruction is organized. If the learner knows what he is expected to learn, he can apply special strategies to

Rules of the Game

I will think of a 3-digit number,
like 234 or 681.

Your goal is to figure out the
number in as few steps as possible.

I will pick digits from 1 to 8. Notice
that 0 and 9 are not included.

My number will NOT use repeated digits.

For each digit that is correct and in
the correct position, I will draw a ★.

For each digit that is correct but in
the wrong position, I will draw a ☆.

If no digits are correct in your guess,
I will write ZILCH.

If all of the digits are correct, I
will draw 3 filled stars, ★★★.

FIG. 3.9   Information overload: too many rules in a single display. (From computer-assisted instruction lesson, *Game of Logic.* Copyright © 1979 by The Board of Trustees of the University of Illinois. Reprinted by permission.)

accomplish the goal. If he knows that he must memorize a long string of numbers, such as 61801–2799, he can make the memory task easier by organizing the numbers in "chunks" (sixty-one, eight-o-one, twenty-seven, ninety-nine) rather than as a string of individual digits. If the learner is studying proverbs and is told that he will have to repeat them verbatim, he can rehearse them by saying them over and over to himself. If the goal is only to identify the meaning of the proverbs, this strategy will not be invoked. Telling learners what to expect will help them to employ an appropriate learning strategy.

Share your instructional plan with the learners. If a student knows what the content of the instruction will be, he can prepare for it by recalling related knowledge. A message about the next instructional event (Fig. 3.11) enables him to generate a framework for understanding and attending to critical aspects of succeeding displays.

Sharing the instructional plan is also helpful if the lesson changes to a new method of presentation. For example, suppose you have been teaching certain rules by first presenting the rule and then giving the examples. In order to relieve the monotony, you decide to shift to giving some examples first and then giving the rule. Tell the students about the change. Another example: A simple word, "DIRECTIONS," at the top of the display informs the student that here is something to learn, not information he is expected to know already. Such an orientation avoids needless confusion.

When introducing a new teaching technique that requires an unusual form of responding, explain the technique and give the student practice in trying it out. Otherwise the student's knowledge could be judged inadequate when the real deficiency is merely an inability to interact with the machine. An orientation to how answers will be judged is also helpful. For instance: "You will be asked to type the missing word in each of 10 analogies. The computer judges typing errors as wrong answers, so check your typing before you ask to have your answers judged."

Use Diagrams Dynamically

CAI lends itself superbly to presenting diagrams as well as verbal text. How do diagrams assist learning? They can convey information that would be

a

```
            Rules of the Game

        I will think of a 3-digit number,
    like 234 or 681.

        Your goal is to figure out the
    number in as few steps as possible.

        I will pick digits from 1 to 8.   Notice
    that 0 and 9 are not included.

        My number will NOT use repeated digits.

        For each digit that is correct and in
    the correct position, I will draw a ★.

        Let's try an example.
    Guess a 3-digit number.  ≫
```

b

```
            Rules of the Game

        I will think of a 3-digit number,
    like 234 or 681.

        Your goal is to figure out the
    number in as few steps as possible.

        I will pick digits from 1 to 8.   Notice
    that 0 and 9 are not included.

        My number will NOT use repeated digits.

        For each digit that is correct and in
    the correct position, I will draw a ★.

        Let's try an example.
    Guess a 3-digit number.   257 ok

    What does the ★ mean? (Type a, b, or c.)

    a) You guessed my number.
    b) The first digit is correct and
       in the correct position.
    c) One of the digits is correct and
       in the correct position.
```

≫   FIGS. 3.10a, 3.10b, 3.10c *(continued)* c   Rules of the Game

                   I will think of a 3-digit number,
              like 234 or 681.

                   Your goal is to figure out the
              number in as few steps as possible.

                   I will pick digits from 1 to 8.   Notice
              that 0 and 9 are not included.

                   My number will NOT use repeated digits.

                   For each digit that is correct and in
              the correct position, I will draw a ★.

                   Let's try an example.
              Guess a 3-digit number.   257 ok

              What does the ★ mean? (Type a, b, or c.)

FIGS. 3.10a, 3.10b, 3.10c   a) You guessed my number.
Presentation of rules of a game   b) The first digit is correct and
interactively. (From computer-   in the correct position.
assisted instruction lesson, *Game* c) One of the digits is correct and
of Logic. Copyright © 1979 by The   in the correct position.
Board of Trustees of the Univer-
sity of Illinois. Reprinted by   ▷ a
permission.)
                                No.   The ★ means that you guessed only
                                1 of the digits in the correct position.

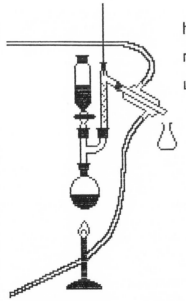

Next we will heat the
mixture so the product
will distill.

FIG. 3.11   Example of keeping the student informed about what to expect. (From computer-assisted instruction lessons, *Introduction to Organic Chemistry.* Copyright © 1980 by Stanley Smith. Reprinted by permission.)

difficult to impart in words only. Diagrams can certainly make the instruction more vivid and actually enable the lesson designer to minimize the amount of verbal explanation.

The Chinese say that one picture is worth a thousand words. An explanation accompanied by an appropriate diagram can explain a concept far better than the verbal text alone. For an example, read the discussion of electrochemical conversion of animal waste to single-cell protein in Fig. 3.12. The text is succinct but somewhat difficult to understand. Now look at Fig. 3.13. Does the addition of the diagram make the text more meaningful? Is the meaning clearer?

As they stand, the text and the diagram could just as well have been presented in a textbook. In CAI it is possible to make the instruction even more effective. Since the text explains a process, you can present the process and explain it one step at a time, allowing the student to control the timing of each successive step (Figs. 3.14a, b, c, d).

Diagrams can make information more vivid. If you read in a geography book that the United States is one-third the size of Africa in land area, you may remember the size difference vaguely. The addition of the diagram with the map of the United States superimposed on Africa makes the factual statement more dramatic and memorable.

There is a question as to whether diagrams should be real pictures or schematic diagrams. Sometimes the details present in a real picture interfere with the student's understanding of the specific concept addressed. Consider carefully whether a detailed picture is necessary. Simple line drawings may be perfectly adequate and perhaps even more facilitative than real pictures. If the instruction does require realism and your CAI system cannot support such pictures, consider using supplementary off-line (not on the computer) materials such as workbooks or slides.

Electrochemical Conversion of Waste to Single Cell Protein

Animal waste is an especially difficult disposal problem because it presents a health danger and an odor nuisance. One solution to the problem is to convert the waste to an innocuous material. To enable the bacteria present in the waste to consume the organic matter, bacterial cells respire and require oxygen. This oxygen can be obtained in situ by electrolysis of water present in the waste. The electricity, in the form of low voltage direct current, separates water molecules into oxygen and hydrogen gases. The bacteria grow rapidly by consuming organic matter and oxygen, producing single cell protein. The hydrogen evolved is a by product. Thus, there are two inputs, animal waste and electricity and two outputs, hydrogen gas and single cell protein.

FIG. 3.12   Verbal explanation of a dynamic process.

Electrochemical Conversion of Waste to Single Cell Protein

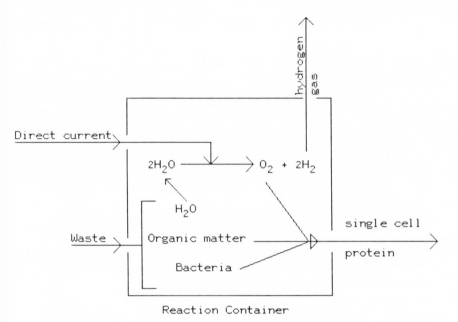

Reaction Container

FIG. 3.13   Schematic diagram to supplement verbal explanation presented in Figure 3.12.

ASK QUESTIONS

The objectives of asking questions during learning are (a) to keep the learner actively engaged and (b) to monitor the learner's understanding. To meet these objectives in CAI, keep these points in mind:

1. The student can answer questions only if the lesson designer has inserted them.
2. Students will not necessarily answer questions unless the lesson requires them to do so.
3. Answering questions is an important part of the learning process, provided that the questions require the student to do some thinking in order to answer them.
4. The questions must be relevant to the content.

An advantage of CAI over other instructional media is that every learner can be required to be actively involved in learning at all times. Some authors

a Electrochemical Conversion of Waste to Single Cell Protein

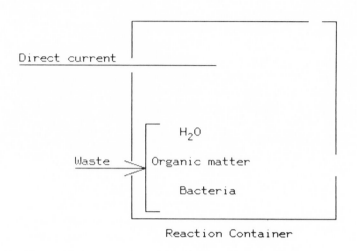

Reaction Container

b Electrochemical Conversion of Waste to Single Cell Protein

Electricity separates water molecules into oxygen and hydrogen.

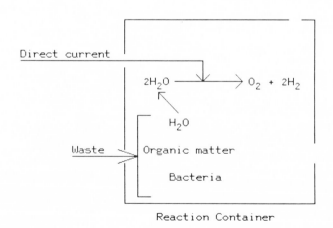

Reaction Container

FIGS. 3.14a, 3.14b, 3.14c, 3.14d   *(continued)*

62

c

Electrochemical Conversion of Waste to Single Cell Protein

Electricity separates water molecules into oxygen and hydrogen.

Bacteria grow rapidly by consuming organic matter and oxygen, to form single cell protein.

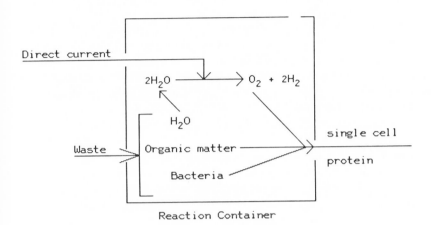

d

Electrochemical Conversion of Waste to Single Cell Protein

Electricity separates water molecules into oxygen and hydrogen.

Bacteria grow rapidly by consuming organic matter and oxygen, to form single cell protein.

The hydrogen evolves as a byproduct.

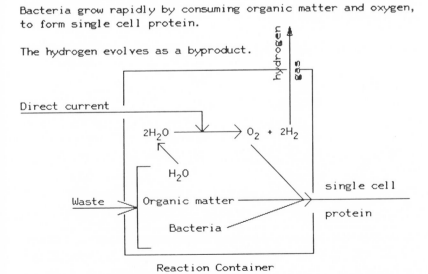

FIGS. 3.14a, 3.14b, 3.14c, 3.14d   Dynamic, student-controlled pacing of step-by-step presentation of the waste conversion process.

erroneously equate being active with actively learning. They write lessons that present one display after another, but do not ask questions to which the learner must respond. The learners are indeed active in such lessons, in pressing keys to move from one display to another, but they may not be learning. Although pressing keys, they may be paying little attention and learning little from what is on the display screens. If you want the learner to be actively learning, ask questions.

However, it is not enough merely to ask questions. Insist that the students respond to them before you display the correct answer. While it is true that a person can actively respond to questions by thinking the answers rather than typing them, you have no way of determining the accuracy of the thinking unless the learner communicates the response overtly. In fact, you have no way of knowing whether the learner is thinking at all.

Merely answering questions is not a sufficient condition for learning. The questions must require the learner to engage in some meaningful activity.

CARDINAL PRINCIPLE: Ask questions that require cognitive processing of the content presented. In order to answer such questions, the learner has to read and understand the presentation.

The objective of the questions is to help students learn the content, not simply to fill in blanks. To obtain meaningful learning, the questions must require that learners do more than merely copy the answer from another part of the display or generate answers from their general knowledge.

Suppose you are teaching the concept *mean*. In the following example compare Questions A and B for the extent of meaningful processing required. Example:

Definition of MEAN

The mean of a set of N scores is the sum of the scores divided by N. You have the following set of scores: 9, 9, 7, 5, and 6.

Question A:

Which of the following defines the mean?

a. $9 + 9 + 7 + 5 + 6$
b. 9
c. 5
d. $(9 + 9 + 7 + 5 + 6) \div 5$

Question B:

The sum of the scores divided by the number of scores is called the _____.

To answer Question B, the student simply has to copy the word *mean*. To answer Question A, the learner must recognize an application of the definition. Therefore, Question A is an example of meaningful processing.

Be sure the student has to read the presentation in order to answer the question. Read the following questions and compare them for the demands they make of the learner.

Question A:
Compute the mean of the set of scores: 9, 9, 7, 5, and 6.
Question B:
The mean is $(9 + 9 + 7 + 5 + 6) \div 5 =$ _____.

In order to answer Question A, the student must read the rule for computing the mean and apply it. To get the answer to Question B, all he has to do is the arithmetic; he does not have to read the rule.

Questions must be relevant to the subject being taught. If students are learning to read the notes on the musical scale, ask about the notes. Don't stop along the way to ask about the number of counts to a quarter note, just because you have chosen to employ quarter notes in the drill. Such a question does not determine what the student knows about the names of the notes.

In order to monitor students' understanding, write questions that will demand this information. A question such as "Do you understand? Type yes or no," tells you only the student's opinion, which may or may not accurately reflect his knowledge. The student may say yes just to get on with the lesson. Some students are not experienced enough to know whether they truly understand.

The format of questions must obviously be chosen to evaluate adequately the extent to which each learner has reached the goals of the unit. If the goal is to recognize an answer, multiple-choice is often a suitable question format. If the goal is to recall or to generate an answer, multiple-choice format may be unsatisfactory, and an open-ended question is called for.

Although consistency with goals is of primary importance, ease of entering responses must also be considered. For example, in most CAI systems students respond to questions by typing. Since most people are not proficient typists, questions should be formulated so that the learner can respond with a minimum of typing. The goal of the questions is to monitor the students' knowledge, not to test their typing skills. If a multiple-choice question will assess learning as well as a long written response, use multiple-choice. For example, suppose the student needs to practice arranging sentences in logical sequence. You present four or five sentences in random order and ask the student to arrange them in logical order. You could ask the student to type the sentences, thus requiring a lot of typing, which is not the skill being taught and is difficult for some students. An alternative is to number the sentences and ask the student to choose which sentence number he wants first, second, and so on. The computer can then display each sentence in the order selected.

This is not to suggest that you sacrifice the quality of the questions for the sake of easy responding. Be aware however, that learners will be responding to questions by typing, and not everybody knows how to type.

How many displays, or how much text should be presented before asking a question? That depends on the maturity of the students and the complexity of the material. One objective of asking questions is to be sure that the student is not just looking at the displays without actually processing or thinking about them. A second objective is to be sure that the student is not only actively attending to the material but is also comprehending it correctly and completely.

Summary

Guidelines for writing the script:

1. Give major attention and time to writing the script. Make it concise, precise and explicit. Initially, present minimum, yet sufficient instruction.
2. Make the presentation consistent with the goals and the target population.
3. Be sure the students know what is going on. Tell them.
4. Use the interactive capability of CAI.
5. Ask questions that require meaningful processing.

PROGRAM AND EVALUATE

Now you are ready to leave the band of circles in the Ripple Plan and actually produce the presentation. Write the computer program for the lesson as planned thus far. Test it yourself as if you were the student; ask a student or a colleague to do the same.

The purpose of early testing is to get a preliminary evaluation of the adequacy of the presentation and the range of possible responses other than the ones you anticipated, both right and wrong. (Early testing also provides an opportunity to see how the program will look on the screen early in lesson development.)

Take notes about the comments students make. Keep a record of any displays and questions that cause consternation or outright misinterpretation. Record unanticipated responses, both correct and incorrect. Notice whether students are able to interact readily with the computer or whether difficulties arise when they are trying to enter responses.

Analyze unanticipated responses. Those that are correct can be added to the list of acceptable responses when you revise the lesson in the next circle of the Ripple Plan. Analyze those that are incorrect to determine the reasons for the errors. If the learner responds that $3 \times 4 = 7$, you can infer that the learner has confused multiplication and addition. Decide if more or different instruction is needed. If a response seems to be totally wrong, interview the student to determine the line of thinking that led to this response. The response might have been wrong because the question was ambiguous and the student interpreted it differently than you had intended. Perhaps the difficulty arose in understanding the text. Use the information gathered as a guide for planning revisions and improvements for the unit.

SAMPLE LESSON

Here we develop the presentation of a unit for our sample lesson, engineering calculations. Now we are at the inner circle of the Ripple Plan, the presentation.

The two topics chosen for this section, mathematical notation and arithmetic operations with units, are taken from the earlier analysis. The first step is to generate the specific goals of this unit, using the detailed task analyses as a guide: the learner will (1) identify the units part of measured quantities, (2) write units in mathematical notation, and (3) perform arithmetic operations with units and with measured quantities.

Next choose an instructional technique. The general goals of the lesson and the specific goals of this unit serve as guides for the choice. Since the goal is to review concepts taught in class and to provide guided practice, a tutorial technique seems most efficient; that is, the lesson will "tell and ask."

For each specific goal, write the instruction and the question(s) the student should be able to answer.

To meet the first goal (identify units part of measured quantities), the script should state that measured quantities are described by units as well as numbers. Since units may be linear or not, the instruction must include diverse examples of both. To generate examples, analyze the critical and variable characteristics of units. The critical characteristic is that they are measures. The variable characteristics are the dimension measured (for example, length, weight) and the linearity/nonlinearity. That is, units may be a single measure like feet or an arithmetic relationship between measures like feet per second. Generate scripts that present both linear and nonlinear examples, and that include diverse instances of nonlinear, such as products and ratios.

Formulate questions that test the ability to identify nonlinear as well as linear units (Displays 1, 2 and 3).

The frequency of asking questions is guided by the complexity of the concept. The concepts here are simple for the target learners, so each concept can be completely presented on a single display. Therefore, questions can be asked on the same display that presents the concept or, if space does not

---

We use both units and numbers to measure quantities.
We say a desk is 6 feet long rather than 6. The unit is
feet.

Pause

We say a bag of apples weighs 2 kilograms. The unit is
kilograms.

Pause

What is the unit in the quantity 3 meters?

Display 1

Units may be linear terms, such as inches or ounces.

Units may also be nonlinear. They may express a relationship, such as a product or ratio. For example, we say
an area is 27 square feet.

Pause

The unit of the area is square feet.

Pause

The unit may be a ratio between two dimensions, such
as miles per hour. Suppose a car is traveling at a speed of
55 miles per hour.

Pause

The unit is miles per hour.

Display 2

Name the units in each of the following:

35.8 cubic centimeters

Pause

10 feet per second per second

Pause

2.54 centimeters per inch

Display 3

---

permit, on the next display. If two or three successive displays were required
to present a concept, asking questions could be postponed until after the
second or third display. However, as a rule of thumb, it is not a good idea
to present more than three displays before asking a question.

The number of questions is determined by the learners' prerequisite
knowledge and the breadth of the concept. Since the target learners are ex-

pected to be familiar with linear units, ask only one question about linear units (Display 1). To satisfy the goal of identifying nonlinear units, questions should include measured quantities with three different representations of units: products, ratios of linear measures, and ratios of linear and nonlinear measures (Display 3).

The second goal is to write units in mathematical notation. Following the procedure for the first goal, the script and questions are presented in a single display (Display 4).

Nonlinear units can be expressed in mathematical notation.

miles per hour $= \dfrac{\text{miles}}{\text{hour}}$

Pause

cubic centimeters $= cm^3$

Pause

feet per second per second $= \dfrac{\text{feet}}{\dfrac{\text{sec}}{\text{sec}}}$

Pause

Write in mathematical notation:
   inches squared

Pause

pounds per square foot

Pause

grams per cubic centimeter

Display 4

To meet the third goal (perform arithmetic operations with measured quantities) the student must be able to do arithmetic with units alone (Display 5) and know the rule that the operations with units precede operations with numbers (Display 6). When generating Display 6, change the format in order to add variety and relieve monotony. Rather than giving a complete explanation and then asking questions, have the learner interact with the computer and participate in solving the example problem during the explanation. Another reason for making this shift in presentation is that, by this point, the learner will probably no longer need the same amount of detail as in preceding displays. Display 7 presents questions that test achievement of the third goal.

The questions generated for Display 7 raise other questions for the author. Should the learner actually cancel quantities on the display? How? It is easy enough to assign a key to the function of drawing a line, but how

We do the same multiplication and division operations with units as with numbers. You can multiply
units:

$$feet \times feet = feet^2$$

You can cancel units:

$$\frac{miles}{\cancel{hour}} \times \cancel{hours} = miles$$

Simplify the following:

$$\frac{feet}{sec^2} \times sec =$$

$$ft.^3 \div ft.^2 =$$

$$\frac{lb.}{in.^2} \div \frac{lb.}{in.^3} =$$

Measured quantities have numbers as well as units. To
do the arithmetic of measured quantities, first do the
arithmetic with units, then with numbers.

$$\frac{12 \ lb.}{gal.} \times 6 \ gal. =$$

What will the units be in the answer?

What will the numerical value be?

Simply the following:

$$100 \ lb. \div \frac{50 \ lb.}{ft.^3} =$$

$$50 \ kg \times \frac{1000 \ g}{kg} =$$

would the computer know where to draw the cancel line? It would be easy if the learner could touch the screen; he could touch the terms to be cancelled. It cannot be assumed that learners will have a touch device, so plan that they will have to type all responses. One solution is to carry on a dialogue with the learner:

Which term do you want to cancel?
Where is the term? Type n for numerator, d for denominator.

Such an interaction would be cumbersome. Try to think of an alternative. How about asking the learner to cancel mentally and simply state the units of the answer? Choose the latter alternative for two reasons: (1) The target students know how to cancel and don't need to practice the physical task of drawing the lines. Their goal is to know that they can cancel with units as well as numbers. (2) It is easier to program the latter. Follow the principle of beginning with a "lean" version of the lesson. If the lesson turns out to be too lean and the students do need to cancel terms on the display screen, the unit can be revised.

At this point, write the computer program for the lesson. Applying the guidelines presented earlier, display only one paragraph at a time. Program the computer so that the learner has to press a key (for example RETURN) to indicate readiness for the next part of the display. If more than one question is to be presented on a display, program the computer to show only one question at a time (Display 3).

We have indicated (with the word *Pause*) the places on the script where the computer waits for the learner to press a key before displaying the next part of the display.

Test the lesson as if you are the student and ask someone else (a student or colleague) to do the same. This testing, or evaluation, leads to questions that must be answered and decisions that must be made to improve and expand the lesson.

A scenario of the evaluation.   One student responded "m" (the abbreviation for meters) to the question in the first display; the computer judged the answer wrong. One student typed a whole sentence, "The unit is meters." This answer was also judged wrong by the computer program. Were those answers really wrong?

An incorrect response on Display 3 was "feet per second" rather than "feet per second per second." Did this error occur because of inadequate instruction or because of a failure on the part of the particular student? We have to decide if most students or only a few will make this error, given the instruction as it now stands. In this case, the decision was not to elaborate the instruction until after more students had tried it. For the time being, we planned simply to write feedback to the error.

On Display 4, the student did not know how to enter the superscript for in.^{2}. What should be done about this problem? Think about some possible solutions. The resolution of this difficulty appears in the next chapter, "Responses and Feedback."

In Displays 5 and 7, students had no problem cancelling and gave the correct units of the answer. Therefore, assume that they don't actually have to draw the lines. However, the first response in Display 6 was the numerical rather than the units part of the answer. Since the number was correct, the learner was confused about why it was not accepted. Always add specific feedback for such an incorrect answer.

Now you are ready to return to the band of circles in the Ripple Plan and continue on to the middle one, "Responses and Feedback."

4 Ripple Plan: Responses and Feedback

You are now at the middle circle of the Ripple Plan, Responses and Feedback. The purpose of this circle is to expand the lesson by adding flexible response judging and feedback, and by revising the presentation in terms of the previous evaluation. Students' responses are discussed first, followed by a discussion of the computer's feedback and remediation. These concepts are then illustrated by applying them to the sample lesson on engineering calculations.

One of the unique features of CAI, and one of its most promising instructional characteristics, is its interactive capability. Each student can be required to respond to each question. The computer, in turn, can be programmed to react to each response with an individualized message. This message, called *feedback,* can be far more than a judgmental expression such as "Right" or "Wrong." The feedback can inform the student why the response is wrong and/or how to get the correct response. Suppose, for example, that the computer displays a triangle and tells the student, "Type the name of this figure." If the student's response is "rectangle," the computer may reply, "No. A rectangle is 4-sided. This figure is 3-sided." If the student's response is "tringle," the computer's feedback might be, "The correct spelling is triangle."

In order to prepare for such an individualized interaction between the learner and the computer, the author must make a number of decisions and plans about students' responses. These plans for student responses fall into three broad categories: (1) choosing the conditions for responding, (2) helping students enter responses, and (3) judging students' responses. For example, decide if the student will be required to respond before seeing the correct answer. Will responses be timed? If students will have to enter special characters, such as π (pi), plan to provide instructions for how to enter the characters. Plan to make the computer program flexible in response judging, that is, to accept all correct responses and reject incorrect ones.

STUDENT RESPONSES

Conditions for Responding

Requirements for responses.   The objective of asking questions and demanding responses during the lesson is to help students process and learn the material. If they know that they can ask to see the correct response before answering a question, they often will not bother to study the lesson. Early CAI studies have shown that some authors allowed students to obtain correct responses to questions without answering them first. Students simply went through the lesson just asking for the answers without bothering to respond at all. Some students probably learned the material; many probably did not. In any case, there was no point to using CAI if the author did not expect the students to study interactively. A textbook with an answer sheet would have been equally successful.

CARDINAL PRINCIPLE: Be sure students make a response before revealing the answer.

Several management decisions must be made in conjunction with this response principle in order to make it viable. If learners give an incorrect response, at what point should the computer display the correct one? If the correct answer is always displayed immediately after every incorrect response, what is to prevent students from entering just any answer at all in order to satisfy the CAI requirement of making a response before seeing the correct one? Students quickly learn to outwit the computer! For this situation, requiring a response does not serve the intended purpose of helping students learn the content. At the other extreme, if the learners are allowed to keep entering responses until they get the right ones, responding may turn into a guessing game. Students may even fail to get the right answer. Again, in this situation, the principle of requiring responses fails to accomplish its goal. Thus, you must not only require responses but must also guide the student toward appropriate responses. Proper management of responses is discussed in chapter 5.

Requirement to enter the correct answer.   If the student enters an incorrect response, should he be required to type in the correct one after the computer displays it? That decision depends on your estimate of the amount of learning that would take place by this requirement. In a multiple-choice question, it is hard to believe that the student will learn very much if he must type a correct response which is just a letter, say *b*. Similarly, if there are only two alternatives such as yes and no, and the student picks the wrong one, there does not seem to be a good reason for asking him to type in the correct response. Merely copying the answer has a low probability of being effective for learning. However, there are situations in which the student finds it helpful to copy a response, as when learning correct spelling. The best way to test the effectiveness of the latter procedure is to present the question again at a later point in the lesson.

Automatic or student-initiated response judging.   In many CAI systems, answer judging may be initiated by either the student or the computer. The lesson author must decide whether to have the computer judge the response automatically or to have the student press a special key like RETURN or NEXT to tell the computer she has finished entering the answer and is ready to have it judged. It is best to maintain a consistent procedure across CAI lessons. Generally, the student is allowed to initiate response judging. For open-ended questions, responses are of such different lengths that it is impossible to be sure how long students' answers will be. For responses that require just one keypress, as for multiple-choice questions, student-initiated judging enables the student to change his mind or to correct a typographical error. There are situations, however, when the student will not be able to overcome a previous habit of successive responding without intervening events, as in counting. Then the student will not press a special key after each response, even if the instructions are explicit to do so. What happens in such cases is that he bends over the keyset busily entering responses without glancing up at the display.

Suppose the student is counting by 2's. He enters a succession of responses without pressing an additional key, such as comma, space, or judging key (for example, RETURN), to separate the responses. Imagine the learner's consternation when he finally looks up and sees all of the digits displayed as one long number:

24681012141618

rather than a succession of 1- and 2-digit numbers:

2   4   6   8   10   12   14   16   18.

For such cases it is best to be practical. Arrange the lesson to anticipate the student's spontaneous mode of operation and judge automatically, rather than forcing the student to initiate judging just for the sake of consistency.

In some CAI systems the computer automatically judges the student's response after every single keypress. For example, in an addition problem when the student enters the digit 2, the computer judges it right or wrong:

$$
\begin{array}{r}
45 \\
+\ 18 \\
\hline
2
\end{array}
$$

If the response is wrong, the computer simply erases it. If the erasure is done too quickly, the student may not have time to look up from the keyboard and may miss seeing it happen. When she does look up, there is no number visible; she assumes that her response was not received by the computer and tries again to enter the same incorrect response. Therefore, you must allow time for the student to see what is happening. If your strategy is to erase the incorrect response, either allow time for the student to see what is happening or else leave a message stating that her answer was received but erased: "2 was incorrect."

Timing responses.   This section discusses timing responses. Timing in presentation of displays is discussed in chapter 6.

In CAI it is possible to limit the time you allow students to respond. Experienced CAI lesson authors have differences of opinion about timing. Some feel the students should be allowed as much time as they need to respond; others feel that the time should be limited in order to keep students alert and the lesson moving along. For some subjects, such as arithmetic facts, knowledge involves speed as well as accuracy. The knowledge must be applied quickly because it will be needed as a tool later. In other types of learning, speed may not be critical. If the students are learning some new principles, they may not respond immediately because they want to study the text more carefully; some are slower-than-average readers. Sometimes learners just sit staring at the terminal because they don't know what to do; sometimes they take time off to talk to a friend or to get a drink of water. The fact is that the lesson author has no way of determining why a particular student is taking an unusual amount of time to respond.

Consider the following points when deciding whether to time responses:

1. Decide if speed as well as accuracy is one of the goals. If it is, time the responses. Be sure to tell the students that questions will be counted as wrong if they are not answered within the specified time.

2. If the subject matter is new and/or relatively complex for the target population, allow them as much time as they need.

3. If the responses require more typing than one or two keypresses and if the target learners ar not particularly good typists, do *not* time the responses.

4. If the target learners need reminders or assistance to maintain concentration, timing mechanisms can be helpful. If a student does not enter a response after a fixed length of time, ask her (on the display screen) if she

needs help, or just automatically present a help sequence. An alternative is an audio reminder to enter a response.

Helping Students Enter Responses

Choosing response forms.   Three factors guide the author when choosing the form of response:

1. the goals for the learner;
2. the ease with which the student can enter the response; and
3. the flexibility of the computer in response judging.

Most important, as noted earlier, is that the questions and hence the response requirement meet the goals of the unit. However, if it is possible to write questions in more than one format, choose the format that also satisfies the two other criteria for response forms: (1) students should be able to enter responses easily, and (2) the computer program should be able to accept all correct responses and reject all incorrect ones.

Multiple-choice questions are convenient in CAI because responses require a minimum of typing. In addition, it is easy to program computers to judge multiple-choice responses. Unfortunately, multiple-choice questions are not satisfactory for every learning goal. If the goal is to recall or apply information or to solve a problem, open-ended questions may be required. Answer judging is more difficult for such questions and requires considerable skill on the part of both the lesson author and the programmer. Such answer judging is discussed in more detail in the section, "Judging Students' Responses."

Specifying desired response form.   Sometimes the lesson author presents a question in such a way that the desired format of the response is not obvious to the student. The author anticipates one format and the student enters another. For example, compare the questions in Fig. 4.1a and Fig. 4.1b for clarity of the desired response.

In Fig. 4.1a, the student's natural reaction might be to type ½ even though it is a multiple-choice question. The lesson author, however, expects the response to be "1," the number of the correct choice. The student who responds "½" is judged wrong and is needlessly frustrated. The question in Fig. 4.1b is better in two ways. First, the lesson specifies the format, or alternative answers. Second, the alternatives are letters rather than numbers, thus avoiding potential confusion between the numerical value of the response and the number that identifies the response.

Questions that require multiple responses also need special consideration. Suppose the learner is asked, "Name three states in New England." Com-

Which of the following is equal to .5?

  1. 1/2
  2. 2/1
  3. 1/5
  4. 1.5

FIG. 4.1a   Amgibuous directions for entering the response. Is the desired response "1"
or "1/2"?

Which of the following is equal to .5? (a, b, c, or d)

  a. 1/2
  b. 2/1
  c. 1/5
  d. 1.5

FIG. 4.1b   Precise directions for entering the response.

pare Fig. 4.2a and Fig. 4.2b and decide which is the better presentation.

In Fig. 4.2a the student's first response will be displayed at 1. After he
presses the RETURN key to indicate he has finished entering the first response, he enters the second response and it will appear next to the 2, and so
on.

Both displays tell the learner how to respond, but the display in Fig. 4.2a
is better than in Fig. 4.2b. Students are accustomed to pressing a key (for
example, RETURN) after each response. The format of Fig. 4.2a enables
them to do so whereas that of Fig. 4.2b does not. The latter asks them to insert commas, which they are not accustomed to doing. Students do not always read the directions, even those that are explicitly stated.

Multiple responses present an additional problem, deciding whether to
judge each answer as it is entered or wait until after all of the answers are inserted. If you judge the responses as the student inserts them, make it clear

Name three states in New England. Press RETURN after each response.

  1.
  2.
  3.

FIG. 4.2a   A reasonable format for entering multiple responses to a question.

Name three states in New England. Type commas to separate your answers.

FIG 4.2b   A nonstandard response format may cause the learner needless difficulty.

to the student whether to replace the incorrect answer with a correct one immediately or to continue on and complete the rest of the question. If the order, that is, the sequence in which responses are given, is irrelevant (as it is in Fig. 4.2) the responses should be accepted as correct, regardless of the order in which they are entered. Maine, Vermont, and New Hampshire, for example, is just as correct as Vermont, New Hampshire, and Maine.

Placing a response.   Some lesson authors ask questions that require the student to fill in blanks embedded in a body of text. Filling in the blanks is an acceptable form of questioning if the blank is at the end of a sentence or in a position where it is easy to see. However, if the blank is buried in a body of text, the students may find it difficult to see where the blank occurs. Furthermore, if the student's response is embedded in the text, it is difficult to place the feedback near the response.

Entering responses.   Two topics are discussed here: (1) alternate response modes, and (2) keys for nonstandard characters.

In some CAI systems students can enter responses by touching the display with a finger or light pen or by manipulating some paddles or a "joy stick," as well as by pressing keys. The mode chosen depends on the subject matter, the target population, and the probability that appropriate hardware equipment (for example, paddles) will be available. If you want the student to identify a particular location, touch mode may be most suitable. For example, in a memory skills game, the goal is to recall the locations of pairs of cards that have the same pictures (Fig. 4.3). The cards in Fig. 4.3 could have been numbered or lettered and the student could have typed the response.

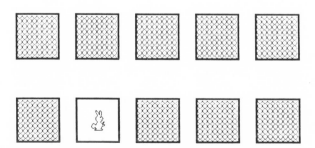

FIG. 4.3   Use of touch to identify locations of cards. (From computer-assisted memory skills lesson. Copyright © 1978 by Control Data Corporation. Reprinted by permission.)

However, doing so would have been difficult for the children for whom this lesson was designed, since many of them did not yet know the letters and numbers. (The message in Fig. 4.3 was presented via audio disk.) Touch or some other manipulative method is also best if you want to allow students total freedom to rearrange things on the display screen. Suppose the task is to arrange a list of words in columns, by categories (Fig. 4.4). The student can simply touch each word in the list and touch the place where he wants it to appear, avoiding the need to type. For some populations, such as the physically handicapped, typing may be exceedingly cumbersome compared to touching.

Some guidelines for use of touch response mode are presented here for those authors using the PLATO CAI system, in which the student enters a response by touching the display screen with a finger. Children tend to rest

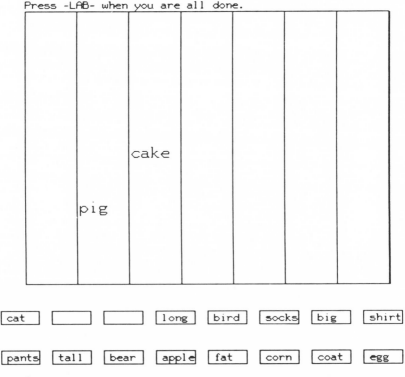

FIG. 4.4   Use of touch to reorganize words from random listing to categories, in columns. (From a computer-assisted instruction lesson for memorizing categorized lists. Copyright © 1979 by The Board of Trustees of the University of Illinois. Reprinted by permission.)

their wrists against the bottom of the display screen, causing the computer to react as though a response was entered although none was intended. This problem can be partially overcome by requiring responses to be made on the bottom third of the screen. Another problem that occurs with learners of all ages is the tendency to drag a finger across the screen on the way to touching the desired location or to wave a finger about while making a decision. The computer detects a touch that the student did not intend and judges the response wrong. The solution to this problem is to teach the student how to enter a response. Tell the student to tuck the thumb under all the fingers and then extend the forefinger for touching.

For microcomputer systems a light pen can be employed to touch the display screen. There is no reason to believe that students have any particular problems with this mode of communication. However, light pens are auxiliary rather than standard equipment for microcomputer systems. Before creating a lesson that requires light pens, determine whether they will be available for your target population.

Keys for nonstandard characters.   Sometimes a lesson requires the student to use the standard keyset to enter nonstandard characters, such as scientific symbols and the letters of foreign languages. For example, some foreign languages, such as Russian, Hindi, and Hebrew, use different characters than English. It is a good idea to assign keys to symbols so that they have a mnemonic or visual relationship. For example, assign to the key K, the letter in the foreign language that sounds like K. It is obvious that you must introduce students to the keyboard of the nonstandard characters. Tell them the devices you have employed to make it easier to remember the appropriate keys, like the sound-alikes noted above. Since some letters in other languages have neither visual nor phonic counterparts in English, the assigned keys are hard for students to remember. If space permits, keep these letter-keypress pairs displayed at all times (Fig. 4.5). Furnish practice through an introductory lesson to familiarize students with the alternate characters displayed by the keys. After the introduction, provide an easy way for students to access a chart to look up characters they may have forgotten.

In science lessons students often need to use nonstandard characters, such as π (pi). Responses also may require superscript or subscript entries, such as H_2O. More than one keypress may be required to enter such responses, such as a shift or special control key. If entering these responses causes difficulties for the learners, step them through the keypress procedure before they actually need to use it.

Judging Students' Responses

Flexibility.   A teacher in a classroom has the advantage of a vast store of knowledge from which to draw, in judging the correctness of a student's re-

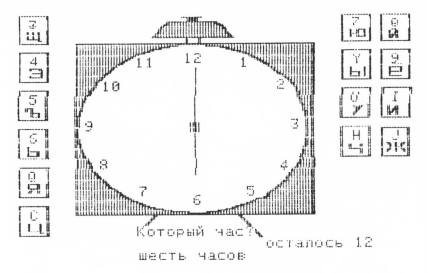

FIG. 4.5   Squares provide memory aid for hard-to-remember keys for Russian characters. (From *Russian Time Lesson, Foreign Language Review Packets for the Microcomputer.* Copyright © 1983 by Constance O'Hara Curtin. Reprinted by permission.)

sponse. An instructor is aware of synonyms, abbreviations, or other expres-
sions that are not exactly the responses expected but are nonetheless reasonable and acceptable. The lesson designer must make such a store of knowledge available in the computer program. The computer must be programmed to analyze every response to ascertain if it is basically correct. Students report that one of the most irritating aspects of CAI lessons is the lack
of flexibility in accepting all correct responses.

The following discussion presents many specific suggestions for flexible
response judging. Until recently it was difficult to implement these recommendations on microcomputer systems. Now, however, programs are available (some for the APPLE II) that extend the BASIC language and provide
the author with the needed commands. One such program was employed to
generate the response judging in the sample lesson on engineering
calculations.

Synonyms or equivalent phrases.   If questions can be correctly answered
by synonyms or equivalent phrases, the computer must be programmed to
accept them. Consider the question, "What is the unit of measure in the expression '6 miles'?" Most students would probably answer, *miles,* but each
of the following is correct and might be given: *mi., mi,* and *mile.* Each
should be accepted as correct.

Numerical responses.   The same flexibility should be allowed in judging
numerical responses. The response .750 should be just as acceptable as 3/4

unless the author specifically requests that the response be given as a fraction. Tolerance should be allowed in cases where a student must give an estimate, say, of the length of a line. Students might actually compute the value of an expression such as $\pi \times 6^2$ and give the answer as 113 rather than write the expression itself. The value to three decimal places is 113.097. The author should decide how much tolerance is acceptable, perhaps from 113.00 to 114.00.

Extra words.   Suppose you have the arithmetic problem: "John has 3 marbles and Jim has 4. How many marbles do they have in all?" You may expect only the numerical response, 7, but is it wrong if the student writes 7 marbles? The computer must be ready to accept this response. Of course, you could tell the student to enter only a number. The problem is that students do not always read the instructions carefully, so it is best to program the computer to ignore extra words. Open-ended questions are also likely to generate responses with extra words. If you ask for the name of a shape, the student may respond, "It is a triangle." With simple material of this sort, avoid the problem of extra words by typing in the sentence and leaving a blank for the student to fill:

"This is called a _____."

In instances where it may be difficult to formulate the question to avoid the problem of extra words, the computer program must be flexible enough to ignore them.

Spelling and typing errors.   Students who know the correct answer to a question may misspell it or make a typographical error. A common error is inserting extra spaces: United   States. Another common typing error is interchanging two letters, as in "objcetive." Extra spaces certainly do not make a response incorrect, nor does a misspelling indicate that the learner does not know the answer to the question. There is a vast difference between a misconception and a misspelling; the computer program must be able to recognize misspellings.

Grammatical errors.   A student might enter a singular response when a plural is expected, as in the following analogy:

$$\frac{\text{fingers}}{\text{hand}} = \frac{\quad}{\text{foot}}$$

A student might respond "toe" rather than "toes." Since the objective of the question is to generate an appropriate analogy, the student's response should not be summarily rejected as wrong. You might say, "Your analogy is correct, but you should use the plural since 'fingers' is plural. Try again."

Exact responses.   There are cases where the response must be exact in every detail, as in spelling the names of drugs in a pharmacology course. In such cases, explain to the student that an exact response is necessary because it might some day mean the difference between correct and incorrect medication, hence the difference between life and death for a patient.

Smart-aleck responses.   Pioneers in CAI lesson development initially attempted to anticipate every possible incorrect response, even an incorrect one that somebody might try just to see how the computer would handle it. These lesson designers came to the conclusion that such an attempt is a time-consuming, if not impossible, task for the designer. Assume that the individuals doing the lesson are serious and do not try to anticipate or deal with ridiculous responses.

COMPUTER FEEDBACK

Definitions

Feedback is any message or display that the computer presents after the student completes a response. Feedback is used as a generic rather than a technical word here and refers to any communication that the computer gives after a student answers a question. Feedback may be as simple as yes or no; it may be as elaborate as an explanation of why the student's answer is incorrect and how to get the correct answer; it may be animated graphics or a statement of the student's score.

Response-contingent feedback is feedback that is designed to address specific student responses. In a sense, all feedback is response-contingent, since it is given after a student's response. In CAI we are particularly interested in the ability to present feedback to the specific error made by the student. Consider the problem,

$$9° \text{ C} - 2° \text{ C} = \underline{\hspace{1cm}}$$

Figures 4.6a and 4.6b demonstrate response-contingent feedback.

Functions of Feedback

Feedback can serve two functions in CAI: (1) to provide information and (2) to provide motivation.

Feedback as motivation.   Some students are motivated by rewards for correct responses. Feedback can serve as such a reward provided that (1) the students in the target group will be motivated by an external reward and (2)

a $9°C - 2°C = 7$ Student's answer.
     The number is correct but   Computer's
     you forgot to state the units.   feedback.

b $9°C - 2°C = 11°C$ Student's answer.
     No. The number is incorrect.   Computer's feedback.

FIGS. 4.6a, 4.6b   Response-specific feedback.

the feedback you choose is considered a desirable reward by that target group.

It is not the case that "motivating" feedback is either motivating or viewed as desirable by all learners in all lessons. Sometimes learners have their own internal motivation. In such cases, feedback that is intended to motivate does not really do so; it merely takes time, which the learner would rather spend studying the lesson. For example, medical students who are studying a CAI lesson to prepare for certification examinations do not necessarily need clever graphics to motivate them.

In some situations feedback can motivate and encourage learners. The clue to success here is to choose feedback that motivates the target students. Some students like to know how they stand in comparison to the rest of the class. When they work individually in CAI, they lack this information. Feedback about their standing, either in achievement in the particular lesson or in progress through the CAI lessons, is motivational for such students. Young children like to see something happen, such as a horse nodding his head, as feedback to a correct response. Feedback that displays a sense of humor motivates learners.

A word of caution: Do not get so carried away with motivational feedback that the student spends more time being "motivated" than entering responses. For example, in a drill on the equivalence of fractions, the student may take just a second or two to respond to a question such as:

Type $<$ or $>$ to make a true sentence.
1/2_____1/3

The author designs a motivational animation to follow the correct response, an animation that goes on for 30 seconds. It does not seem reasonable for students to devote 25% of their time in the lesson to studying the subject and 75% to being motivated. Maintain your perspective on the function of the motivation when designing it.

In CAI inexperienced authors sometimes think they are motivating learners when they present exuberant praise after each correct response. They make comments, like "Wow, are you ever smart," and even give the student high praise for good work when the student needs three tries and several hints to get the right answer. This type of feedback may be appropriate for specific populations, but for most learners, excessive or phony praise is not motivating. Similarly, elaborate animations that go on for several seconds may be delightful the first time they are encountered, but they lose their charm and their novelty very quickly and make students bored and impatient.

Feedback as information.   Feedback can provide learners with two kinds of information. (1) It can tell the learner if the answer is right or wrong and (2) it can provide corrective information. Sometimes judgmental information (right or wrong) is corrective in itself.

Correct responses.   When the computer judges a response correct, it is providing new information, provided that information is not self-evident to the learner. In many situations students know when their answer is correct. They know they performed correctly when they have reached a goal, like successfully managing the care of a sick patient. They also know when they are finally right after first trying unsuccessfully to recall a word such as a name: "I saw Jane, no, Janet, no, Jenny yesterday at the movies." If learners have a way of knowing that their response is correct, the information provided by the "ok" is merely confirmation that they have performed the task as requested.

In either case, there is no need to write extensive feedback after a correct response, explaining why the response is correct. It serves no useful purpose, and students will not read it. They know why they are correct, or at least they think they do. A simple "Right" or an equivalent is all the informational feedback needed after a correct response.

Incorrect responses.   When an answer is incorrect, feedback should not only inform learners that they are wrong but should also provide corrective information. The purpose of feedback is not just to help learners get a particular answer right; it is to help them overcome errors in understanding.

To write useful feedback you have to figure out (1) why the learner erred, and (2) how to help the learner overcome the misunderstanding.

The corrective feedback can vary from a simple no to an explanation of why the student's response is wrong, and why a particular answer is correct. A simple no and knowledge of the correct response may be adequate feedback for some tasks for certain target populations. For some questions a no automatically tells the learner the correct response. In Fig. 4.7, for example, the student can conclude that if the response "nothing" is incorrect, then "anything" must be correct. However, knowing the correct answer is not the same as understanding the underlying principle. The author has to decide if

Choose the correct word. Type it.
I didn't see (anything) (nothing).

FIG. 4.7   If student responds incorrectly to a two-choice item, feedback No is corrective as well as judgmental information.

students in the target population would benefit from additional feedback. If so, the author should explain why "nothing" is incorrect, and follow with additional exercises to monitor that understanding.

In most cases a no is not sufficient as corrective information. Provide a hint that also tells the learner why the response is wrong (Fig. 4.8). The hint might suggest what to think about to get the correct response. For example, suggest that the student use knowledge from trigonometry about sines and cosines to solve a physics problem.

The amount of feedback depends in part on the pace or flow of instruction you wish to achieve, the response mode, and the role of the question at this point in the instruction. If a question presented within a tutorial dialogue has as its purpose making sure that the student is "keeping up" with the instruction, feedback can be fairly elaborate. If the question is part of a drill, you may prefer to move the student through the drill, giving a minimum of feedback after each question. You might give a hint and allow the student a chance to try again, or you might decide to provide the correct answer. In this case, provide more elaborate remediation only if the student fails to meet a prespecified criterion at the end of the drill.

Effective Feedback

1. Make the feedback response-specific. The feedback should present information that is directed specifically to the student's error. To do so, first analyze the error. If it is a conceptual one, such as the incorrect application of a rule, tell the learner why that response is wrong; or give hints on a correct method; or provide information about why another response is correct. If the error is nonconceptual, such as a misspelling, say so specifically. If the response is wrong because it is not one of the choices, say so.

2. Place the feedback near the response to increase the probability that the student will notice it. Students must notice feedback in order to benefit from it.

4 × 3 = 7   Student's answer.
No. You added; this is a
multiplication problem.   Computer's feedback.

FIG. 4.8   Informative feedback to incorrect response.

3. Keep the question, the student's incorrect response, and the feedback all in view on the display at the same time and thereby draw attention to the feedback by pointing to or underlining relevant parts of both question and response. Doing so also enables the learners to look back at what they did and to learn from their errors. Students can learn from their mistakes if both the question and the incorrect response are available. However, just looking at the incorrect response has little learning value if the question was erased and there is nothing to refer to.

4. Write feedback that the student will understand; if she does not know how to use it, no benefit will be derived. In one computer-presented lesson, first-graders were given the task of generating a strategy for solving a reasoning problem. The feedback, in addition to ok or no, was a record (display) of the problems the student had done earlier, the student's responses, and whether they were right or wrong. The intention was to enable the learner to generate a correct strategy by reviewing his own work and inferring why some responses were correct and others not. This feedback was not effective because the first-graders did not know how to use it.

5. The student must be willing to accept the corrective information. In the reasoning task just described, some students were given an alternate kind of feedback. After each incorrect response, the computer stepped the learner through the correct procedure for solving the problem. This feedback was no more effective than the record of the student's previous work. Although the children followed directions and stepped through the correct procedure, on subsequent problems they reverted to their own spontaneous, incorrect strategy. Since their spontaneous strategies happened to result in correct responses for many problems by chance, they saw no reason to replace their own strategy with that of the computer.

Inappropriate Feedback

Beware of encouraging errors! Designers of CAI lessons for young children often try to communicate feedback nonverbally. Thus, if an answer is correct, the feedback may be a smiling face; if incorrect, a sad face. Sometimes the feedback for incorrect responses is so interesting that students deliberately make mistakes so that they can see it. The classic story is told that in one CAI curriculum development project the feedback for an incorrect answer was an animation of tears coming down a child's face. The students found this animation fascinating and many made mistakes on purpose so that they could see it. Whatever the age of your target population, beware of this pitfall of making feedback for a mistake a rewarding or desirable experience.

Undesirable Feedback

One of the greatest dangers in CAI is that undesirable classroom techniques may be transferred to CAI, where their undesirability is magnified by the computer. An example is the response to wrong answers. In the classroom, having a paper returned with large red checks to signify errors is embarrassing to the student, if not devastating. Chances are that only the student himself sees the paper, or at most the few students who sit near him. However, if a student makes a mistake in a CAI lesson and the feedback is a large red X across the screen, anybody looking in the direction of the terminal can see the error. It will be even more likely to attract attention if the X flashes on and off. Now everybody in the room can see that Johnny made a mistake. This kind of feedback does not help Johnny corrrect his errors; to make matters worse, it is offensive.

Snide or insulting remarks are other forms of feedback that are not only abrasive but do not help the student learn. Comments such as "That's the third time you did it wrong, dummy" interfere with learning. It's not what we had in mind when we referred to response-contingent feedback. In the classroom an instructor might give feedback that on the surface sounds insulting, but the students understand from the gestures that accompany it or from the tone of voice in which it is said that no insult is intended. The student in CAI receives no such cues. What is "cute" or nonconformist but acceptable in the classroom may not be in CAI.

REMEDIATION

What can be done to help a student who either can't answer the questions or makes an excessive number of errors? Feedback to individual incorrect answers does not seem to be sufficient corrective information, and the learner needs more extensive help. Such help is called remediation.

Remedial Loops

A remedial loop is the section of instruction to which students are routed if their performance in the main body of instruction is unsatisfactory. After students complete this remedial loop, they are routed back to the point from which they came.

Content

The remediation may consist of different explanations of the subject matter, more detailed explanations of examples, new example applications, or any instruction that helps students overcome their misunderstandings or their lack of understanding. Sometimes inexperienced CAI authors claim they provide remediation when the remedial loop merely takes students back to the same instruction. In non-CAI settings it has been shown that repetition of the same materials is not as effective as supplementary materials and methods. There is no reason to believe that the situation would be different in CAI. If students do not understand the original explanation, chances are that further explanations or different ones are needed for remediation.

We reject the idea that "practice makes perfect." A prime example is the case of a CAI reading lesson for kindergarten and first-grade children. The goal of the lesson is to teach letter discrimination. In the lesson a covered letter on the display screen is identical to one of two letters shown at the top of the screen (Fig. 4.9). The student's task is to uncover the letter piece by piece until she thinks there is enough information to match it to one of the letters shown at the top. Most of the children simply uncover every part of

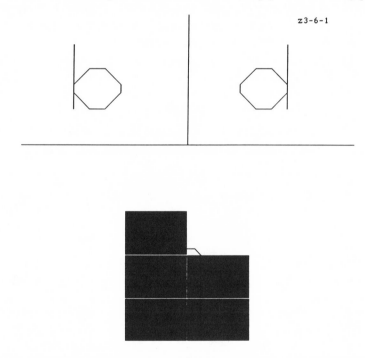

FIG. 4.9   Letter discrimination task. (From computer-assisted instruction lesson, *The Hiding Letter*. Copyright © 1978 by Control Data Corporation. Reprinted by permission.)

the covered letter before matching it to a letter at the top. Even after repeated practice, they fail to get the idea that they should uncover only discriminating parts of the letters. Practice alone does not enable them to learn the problem-solving strategy.

Off-Line Remediation

Of course, remediation need not be provided by the computer (on line). At the end of the lesson, specific off-line, that is, non-CAI remediation, might be recommended. For example, the message may suggest that the student seek assistance by reading some pages in a given book. So, when off-line remediation is used, the student must leave the computer terminal and return at another time. The effectiveness of this procedure depends on the availability of materials and the student's motivation to use them.

If the first testing of a unit of instruction leads you to believe that some learners will need remediation, plan it immediately. Include both the presentation and the questions. Most often it is best to wait until the lesson is completed and a number of students from the target population have tested it before writing remedial loops. It is difficult to gain an accurate picture of the need for remediation based on a sample of just one or two individuals. There is no sense wasting time preparing remediation that will never be used.

PROGRAM AND EVALUATE

After completing plans for response judging and feedback, leave the band of circles in the Ripple Plan to make these additions to the computer program. Also, revise the presentation and questions, as determined by the previous testing.

Test the lesson yourself as if you were the student; ask a student and/or a colleague to do the same. The purpose of this testing is to evaluate the response judging, feedback, and other revisions you made. As before, take notes on difficulties students encounter and on unanticipated responses. Another purpose of this evaluation is to get a preliminary estimate of the difficulty of the particular unit of instruction. This information will help you decide what data-keeping mechanisms you need to add in order to manage the flow of instruction. Can the learners get the right answers after one or two tries, or should you plan to tell the right answer? Will some learners need remediation, and if so, what data will you need for making this decision?

SAMPLE LESSON

Production of the sample lesson on engineering calculations now resumes, at the second circle of the Ripple Plan, Responses and Feedback. The lesson is revised in response to the problems that were encountered in the previous testing. Flexible response judging and feedback are added to the instruction.

The first step is to plan the revisions. The correct answer to the question in the first display is "meters." However, students who tested the lesson gave other correct responses, "m" and "meter." These responses are now added to the list of acceptable answers. The computer should also accept the response, "The unit is meters" as correct. Program the computer to ignore all extra words.

A second problem identified in the first evaluation of the lesson was the difficulty of entering exponents, that is, superscripts. First, consider the possibility of formulating the questions in a different way so that entering the response will be easier. Since the goal of the question is for the learner to generate an answer, rather than just recognize the correct one, the question must ask for a constructed response, one which the student generates. Therefore, retain the original questions, and find a way for the learner to enter the superscripts as easily as possible.

Two ways to solve the superscript problem are: (1) Write the program so that it automatically enters all numbers in the response as superscripts. For example, if the student types, "in2" the computer displays "in^2." (2) Assign a specific key, or pair of keys, such as Control-U, the superscript function. The learner types "in," then the keys Control-U, and then "2," and the computer displays "in^2." This system can also be used for other special needs, such as entering subscripts.

One of the people who tested the lesson earlier entered the incorrect response, "feet per second" rather than "feet per second per second" on Display 3. Infer why the learner erred: he failed to understand that the unit is the entire expression, not just part of it. Add that information as the feedback message, and illustrate it: "The unit is the entire expression: feet per second per second." We also observed that in doing the calculations in Display 6, the student made the mistake of entering the numerical part of the answer when the units part was requested.

$$\frac{12 \text{ lb.}}{\text{gal.}} \times 6 \text{ gal.} =$$

What will the units be in the answer?

Add feedback for this error: "Calculate the units part of the answer first."

Next, program these additions and revisions and evaluate them. Let us consider two different scenarios of what might occur during this testing. Suppose we choose to program the computer to write numbers automatically as superscripts. During the trial run, the student asks how to enter the superscript. Although it was arranged for the computer to enter the numbers automatically as superscripts, this information was not communicated to the learner. Therefore, a message to this effect must be added to the lesson.

An alternate scenario: choose a pair of keys, Control-U, to perform the superscript function and display the following message at the bottom of the screen for the learner's information:

Ctrl-U for superscript

The result of the evaluation: the student does not understand the message and is frustrated when trying to enter the correct answer. This indicates that before displaying the message, the lesson should teach the learner how to enter superscripts.

Next, evaluate the effectiveness of the feedback on "feet per second per second" that was added to Display 3. Several scenarios are possible. The students learning the material this time do not err, so they do not need to see the feedback, and there is no opportunity to evaluate it. Their performance indicates that there is no need to elaborate the instruction. An alternate scenario is that the student in this tryout makes the same mistake about the unit, but responds correctly to succeeding questions on the same topic. Reserve judgment about the need to elaborate instruction until more people have tried it. For the time being, the feedback seems to be adequate, but it will be useful to monitor each learner's understanding of this concept by keeping a record of the number of successive questions the learner answers correctly. If students in later trials make the same mistake and also err on the next question, it will be necessary to elaborate on the instruction and to add more practice.

Now that the Responses and Feedback have been evaluated, return to the circles of the Ripple Plan, this time to the third circle, which deals with Human factors and Management decisions.

5 Ripple Plan: Human Factors and Management

You are now at the outer circle in the Ripple Plan, where the goal is to expand the lesson by making revisions, taking measures to smooth human-computer interaction, and employing features to control the flow of instruction. Human factors include motivation, access to special displays, interaction with the computer, and personalization. Management involves decisions about who will control the instructional path through the unit, and how to regulate those aspects of management that are placed under computer control.

MANAGEMENT UNDER COMPUTER CONTROL

Management decisions affect the student's instructional path within a unit and between units. In the Ripple Plan, decisions concern managing the flow of instruction within the unit. Later, in chapter 6 (lesson development at the overall level), the flow of instruction between units is discussed. Within the unit the following decisions are made: (1) the number of questions to ask, (2) the number of tries to allow for answering each question, (3) criteria for advancing and (4) data to keep.

Number of Questions

How many questions should you ask? The answer depends on the role of the question in the instruction and the complexity of the material. If the concept presented is easy and the purpose of the question is to maintain the student's attention, a single question is sufficient. If, on the other hand, the concept is complex and many-faceted, like rules of punctuation or principles of physics, one question or one practice exercise would not test the learner's understanding adequately. In such cases, present a set of questions.

The number of questions can be based on performance. For example, the criterion may be that the learner must answer five successive questions correctly on the first try. A learner who responds correctly to the first five questions does not have to do any more. One who answers the first two questions right, and then the third wrong, must answer at least five more questions. Students who need more practice must get it. Students who understand the material being taught do not then have to waste time doing a large, predetermined number of exercises. For example, once a learner demonstrates the ability to do long division problems correctly, say five in a row right, there is no need to have him do 20 more. This individualization of practice questions is most appropriate for the application of rules and principles.

An alternative method is to require all learners to do the same fixed number of exercises. This decision is most appropriate when each of the items tests different knowledge, such as translation of vocabulary items. Knowing the first five words in a vocabulary list does not guarantee that the learner knows the others.

Number of Tries

Another management decision is how many times to allow the learner to try to enter the correct response if the first is incorrect. The student can be allowed only one attempt to answer the question. If the response is incorrect, display the correct one. As noted earlier, when this method is routinely used, learners often take the easy way out and type anything, just to satisfy the requirement of making a response. They know full well that the correct one will appear shortly. The same problem can occur if the correct response is displayed after a fixed number of tries, say three. If, on the other hand, students are allowed as many tries as they need to get the correct response, they sometimes engage in a guessing game and lose track of the question to which they are responding. They focus only on getting the blank filled. Do you believe they are learning anything in such a situation?

Fortunately, it is not necessary to make the same management decisions for responses to every question. When determining the number of "tries" to allow, decide first of all if the target learners will benefit from more than one chance to respond. If so, provide the student as much opportunity to generate the correct answer as possible without turning responding into a guessing game. The following are examples of situations where one try is enough. If the content is relatively easy, and the target learner can probably learn from reading the feedback that includes the correct answer, one try is sufficient. If there are only two alternative answers, one try is sufficient because if one answer is wrong, the other must be right. If the task is rote memory or multiple choice, one try is usually sufficient. At most, allow a second try before showing the correct response.

When a question requires non-rote cognitive skills, such as the application of a concept, students may benefit from trying to correct their own errors. In such cases a succession of increasingly informative hints will be useful. Such hints are sufficient for most students.

What do you do for learners who are unable to self-correct, even with the hints? If you don't tell them the answer, they will be "stuck," unable to go on. If you do tell them the answer, they may be advancing in the lesson without adequate understanding. It is better to tell the answer so that the learner can go on; there is no point in studying a lesson that can't be completed. A student can frequently learn if she sees the correct answer after she has answered incorrectly. Sometimes an explanation of why the answer is the correct one is also helpful. To prevent a learner from continuing on without sufficient understanding, monitor her performance on successive questions and concepts.

Criteria for Advancing

A student who is not performing well probably does not understand the unit of instruction. It makes little sense to allow her to continue. Rather, she should be branched to a remedial sequence. What criteria can the author apply to route the student to a remedial loop?

Remediation can be based on the student's ongoing performance, such as the number of successive questions the student answers incorrectly on the first try. If the number exceeds a preset criterion, remediate. An alternative criterion is an end-of-the-unit calculation of the proportion of problems the student answered correctly on the first try. In PLATO jargon these are aptly called "first ok's." If the proportion of first ok's is below some preset criterion, say 75%, the learner is routed to remediation. Since a student may improve his performance as he goes along in the unit, his understanding at the end of it may be better than indicated by the proportion of first ok's. Therefore, for some situations, and end-of-the-unit quiz is a better determinant of the need for remediation.

Data Keeping

In order to manage instruction, the computer must gather data. At this stage of lesson development the data-keeping mechanisms serve two functions: (1) to monitor the learner, and (2) to evaluate the instruction. One useful form of data is the number of tries the student takes to answer a given question correctly. If the learner requires numerous tries, you know not only that he doesn't understand but also that instruction, feedback, and/or the questions need revision. (The computer also makes use of the number of tries to decide when to tell the student the correct answer.)

Similarly, the number of first ok's serves more than one function. In addition to providing a basis for advancing the learner through the unit, it measures the quality of the unit as a whole.

ALTERNATIVES IN ASSIGNING MANAGEMENT

The foregoing discussions may have left the impression that the author makes all management decisions and puts them under computer control. However, alternatives exist and are sometimes chosen. In CAI, the path of instruction may be under the control of the computer, the student, the classroom instructor, or some combination thereof. Before making management decisions for a unit, the author must decide which management decisions to assign to computer control and which to leave to the student and/or the instructor. Some authors make these decisions on the basis of the intuitive assumption that students will learn better if they are in charge of their own instruction. However, intuition can, and has, led many authors astray. The fact that you can allow learner control in CAI does not necessarily mean that it is wise to do so.

Decisions about locus of control of instruction should be based on the results of research and experience. What information do you need to make these decisions?

Learner Control

Why bother with learner control? If the instructional treatment is effective and students perform well, why not present the instruction under computer control? One reason is that computer control is more costly than learner control, both in terms of students' time and of computer resources. In order to control learning, the computer must gather and store a considerable amount of data. Programming code must be written to collect the data, retrieve it, and make decisions about what to do next. The more elaborate the management program, the greater the use of system resources. Thus, if students could perform at the desired level under learner control, computing resources could be saved. If, in addition, students could learn more quickly under their own control, time would be saved.

Many authors believe that allowing students some control of the learning process will improve achievement in terms of increasing motivation, decreasing anxiety, and improving attitude.

Are all of these expectations fulfilled? Do students learn better or faster if given control of instruction? Do their attitudes improve? There is no simple yes or no answer to these questions. The benefit of learner control varies with the extent of control allowed and the ability of the target population to generate appropriate learning strategies in the given subject. Performance is rarely better under learner control, sometimes equally good, and sometimes worse.

Total student control.   The student can be given complete control of all instructional decisions, such as which topics to study, the order in which to study them, the number of exercises to practice, and so on. The author who gives the student all of this control is making the explicit, if not implicit, assumption that the student is the best judge of appropriate learning strategies. This assumption is not universally true.

If the target students are mature learners in the subject area they are studying, they will probably perform as well under learner as under computer control, but may take longer to complete the lesson. Those who have poor learning skills or who are not knowledgeable in the subject matter will perform worse under total learner control because of poor study habits. For example, they don't review concepts that they have missed. They do not manage their time efficiently, so that they frequently do not complete lessons within the given time limit.

Control of one or two variables.   Do students perform better if given control of just one or two instructional variables, such as the sequence of topics or level of difficulty of practice? For the most part, only adults who are high performers in the subject will be skillful managers of the sequence of instruction and will perform equally well (not better) under learner than under computer control. Other students usually perform worse under learner than under computer control. Experience and research are in agreement with common sense. If a student knows little or nothing about a subject, how can you expect her to choose a reasonable sequence of topics?

How about letting students pick the difficulty level of practice exercises? Unfortunately, the situation here is similar. Most students, both adults and children, do not use good judgment when allowed to set the difficulty level; they choose items that are too easy or too hard. As for allowing students to decide how much to practice, there is no definitive answer. Sometimes they practice appropriately, sometimes too much, and sometimes too little.

Control of review.   Authors of lessons for college students often recommend that students be given the option of reviewing instruction or accessing supplementary materials at their own discretion. This recommendation is particularly true of drills or practice lessons that supplement classroom instruction. Good students do use the option to review, and the time spent reviewing does correlate highly with top performance.

Option not to answer.   One of the cardinal principles presented earlier is that students should be required to respond to every question. Sometimes, however, professional students, such as those in veterinary medicine, do not like to be restricted to going through small steps and answering every question when they are sure they know the answer. They want to get on with the lesson as quickly as possible and to spend time studying sections in which they are weak. Their request seems reasonable, particularly if the lesson is intended to be self-checkup or practice, supplementary to other instruction. However, allowing the learner this type of control will succeed only if students are good judges of their own knowledge.

Affective consequences.   Student control can be motivating and attitudes can be positively affected, particularly at the elementary- and secondary-school levels; unfortunately, improved or even equivalent performance does not necessarily result. In fact, sometimes performance is worse. Students do not necessarily care whether they are allowed control of instructional variables.

Control by Classroom Instructors

Beginning authors sometimes decide that learning should be entirely under the rigid control of the computer and based only on a systematic analysis of the content to be taught. This decision may cause difficulties if the lesson is intended to supplement classroom instruction. The student may become proficient in a skill in the classroom before studying the topic in the CAI lesson. Since the computer does not have information about the student's performance in the classroom, the management system will require him to study this topic in the CAI lesson, wasting his time. This problem could be overcome if the lesson author provided an option for the instructor to override decisions made by the computer.

Although a CAI lesson is designed for a specific target population, there are situations in which other target populations can derive some benefit from the lesson, too, if the instructor is allowed the option of changing some of the management parameters. For example, suppose the lesson is generated to stand alone, independent of other instruction. The computer manages instruction so that students study subordinate concepts before learning the higher level concepts. In addition the lesson requires a high level of mastery of each section before a student is allowed to advance. This independent lesson might also be useful as supplementary or remedial study, if instructors can override computer management and assign students to selected topics and selected mastery levels.

Advice and Learner Control

The computer can be programmed to give students advice about what to do next. For example, the lesson may allow them to decide how many problems to practice, but if they seem to be performing above or below some criterion, tThe computer can suggest that they do not need more practice or they need to review or do easier problems, as the case may be. There is no guarantee that students will follow the advice; they may follow it just in part. An advising system is helpful only if students are willing to accept the advice and follow it. Students may set goals for themselves that are not the same as the ones the lesson author sets.

Guidelines

Let us now return to the Ripple Plan to decide which aspects of instruction to place under computer control in the unit under development. First, answer the question, "Does the goal for the overall lesson mandate a specific set of management decisions for all units?" In some environments, such as military and industrial, performance criteria for the units of instruction must fit specifications set for the lesson as a whole. An engine must be repaired exactly right or it simply will not function. A technician must know exactly when to open certain valves and turn others off in order to keep the flow of liquids at appropriate levels. However, college students do not have to get an "A" or "B" in a course in order to pass, even if the instructor has such a goal for all students; the individual students may set their own goals for themselves. In fact, some lessons, such as reviews for students preparing for professional certification examinations, are written to provide extra practice for students who want it.

If the goal of the lesson is to achieve a prespecified standard of performance, place the flow of instruction within the unit under complete computer control. If the lesson is for voluntary study by mature learners, as a supplementary self-check learning tool, plan for learner control.

If decisions for a unit are not predetermined by overall lesson restrictions, ask, "Is the average member of the target population likely to be a good learner?" A good learner is one who monitors his learning and is aware of when he doesn't understand and needs to study more, and knows how to allocate study time efficiently. If the lesson content is easy or if a good learner is a nonnovice in the subject matter, he can be allowed considerable freedom: the option to review previous displays at will, to advance to succeeding displays without meeting a particular standard of performance, to do as few or as many exercises as desired, and to set the difficulty level of exercises.

However, even if the target students are good learners, it is not profitable to allow them control in the unit if they are not knowledgeable in the subject or if the content is not easy for novices. A person who knows how to study physics does not necessarily know how to study a foreign language; a good learner in business administration may find it difficult to study computer science.

Suppose that the target students have average learning skills. Then ask, "Should the content be easy for this population?" In other words, are they apt to learn the material with few errors, the first time through? If so, allow them control tentatively, subject to later evaluation when testing the lesson.

In all other cases, plan to place management under computer control. These are cases in which the learners have poor study skills or are average learners facing content that is not necessarily easy for them.

There are no easy answers to decisions about management. All decisions should be considered tentative, subject to revision after testing with target students.

SMOOTHING HUMAN-MACHINE INTERACTION

In chapter 3 the importance of telling learners what to expect was discussed. It is also important to anticipate possible apprehension and to tell learners how to communicate with the computer.

CARDINAL PRINCIPLE: Tell students what to expect. Don't expect them to be mind readers.

Communicate Nature of Task

An important prerequisite for success in a task is understanding it. A student brings to a CAI lesson his experiences and expectations from traditional instructional modes. If a task, when presented in CAI, is somehow different from the traditional presentation, the student may not perceive this difference and may not understand the lesson as intended by the author. The student will not benefit from lessons that use CAI's unique capabilities if there is a discrepancy between what the author expects and what the student does.

An anecdote will best exemplify this contention. A CAI lesson was created for primary grades, in which each display showed two views of a common object. The pictures differed in one half and not in the other (Figure 5.1). A third picture, which was covered, was purported to match one of them. The child's task was to uncover one, and only one, part of the hidden

One of the camels is hiding under the cover.   #4
Touch the part you want to peek at.

FIG. 5.1   Display from a problem-solving task. (From computer-assisted instruction lesson, *Peek! A Problem-Solving Game.* Copyright © 1978 by Control Data Corporation. Reprinted by permission.)

picture, and on that basis decide which of the views it would match. The strategy, of course, was to uncover the discriminative part. For pictures of the camels, uncovering the part that showed the head provided enough information to know which view would be matched. The lesson contained 12 different pairs of pictures.

In traditional instruction, the materials stay the same from day to day. If the covered picture matches the camel with its head down the first time through the lesson, chances are that the camel with its head down will be the correct match the next time. However, in the CAI lesson the computer generated the graphic displays anew each time a student studied it. The view that would be matched was randomly chosen. Therefore, when the lesson was done a second time, the correct answer might be different than it was previously. When the children began the task for the second time, some of them recalled which views of the pictures had been matched earlier. To quote one 5-year-old, "Oh, I remember. It was that one yesterday," as he pointed to the camel with its head up. He expected to get the right answer on the basis of memory, as he could have done in traditional instruction, and not by generating a suitable strategy. He paid no attention to the usefulness of uncovering part of the covered picture and uncovered the tail. Since he had cast the task in the light of his experience with printed materials, he was totally confused.

CAI presents the additional problem of allaying students' concerns about how they will know what they are supposed to do. You, the author, know that you will provide explanations in succeeding displays, but the students don't. Tell them what's coming. Suppose you will designate certain keys to perform special functions, such as writing superscripts, subscripts, and backspacing, or accent marks for foreign languages. You plan to keep the information about which key does what displayed on the screen at all times. Tell the students this will be the case. If you do not tell them, many learners will sit at the computer terminal copying the information on paper just in case they need to refer to it later. Doing this is a common reaction of students, and such a waste of their time! One sentence telling them that support will be provided saves them time and prevents unnecessary annoyance with the lesson.

Provide Access to Special Sections

A student should be able to access instructions at any point within a unit and return to the place desired without having to restart the entire unit of instruction. Similarly, if a student leaves the problem or question she is working on and branches to some extra help, she should be returned to the problem she was doing. For example, suppose a student is working through a drill in which preceding questions remain on the display. If the student gives a wrong response, the author routes her to another display and provides an explanation. After reading the corrective information, the student is routed back to the drill and has to start all over again from the beginning, repeating all of the questions, even those previously done correctly. Such routing is abrasive and a waste of the student's time. It is easy to program this procedure, but it is totally unacceptable as good lesson design.

Sometimes a student needs information in addition to that given on the display in order to answer a question. He may wish to access definitions, rules, formulas, or the like. In a textbook he can look up such information on another page and mark the place so that he can readily flip to it or keep it in view. In CAI, flipping back and forth between displays is not satisfactory. The flow of the learning process is blocked or lost in the transition between the displays. It is best to present the supplementary information on the display the person is working on. If you want the student to look up a rule, but do not want to have it in view while he uses it, show it on the screen at the student's request. Then erase it as soon as the student starts to enter the response.

Ease Use of Special Keys

Be consistent.   One way of easing student-terminal interaction is to be consistent in the use of keys. Use the same key for the same purpose throughout the unit of instruction. For example, always use the same key (like ENTER or RETURN or NEXT) to initiate answer judging or to go on to the next display. If possible, do not use the same key for two different purposes, such as to access supplementary data and to continue on to the next display.

Give directions.   Give clear, simple directions for use of keys. Be brief, but give enough information so that students can understand the directions. Consider, for example, the following message:

Press space bar for more information.
Press RETURN to go on.

Students who are new to CAI or who are immature learners sometimes do not understand that they should press the space bar only if they wish more information. Consequently they press the space bar and get information that they did not really want. Phrasing the information in the following way avoids this kind of misunderstanding:

If you want more information, press space bar.
If you want to go on, press RETURN.

Some students may need to be told that DATA or RETURN is the name of a key:

If you want more information, press the DATA key.

Provide memory support.   If keys for nonstandard characters or functions are used, such as "°" for degrees or Control-U for superscript, keep the information on display at the bottom of the screen. If there is simply not enough room for such information on the display, allow the student to press a special key to get it when needed.

MOTIVATION

Personalize Instruction

Personalize by including the student's name in the computer's feedback. If you plan to use the student's name, design a display that asks the student what he wants to be called in this lesson. Place this display at the beginning of the unit, or at the beginning of the lesson, so that the name is available for use in other units, too. In some systems the student's name is stored by the computer for record keeping. It is likely to be the entire name, first and last. If the student's name is retrieved from this source, the result may be an unnatural dialogue: "Good work, John M. Smith." Some students, particularly those in elementary school, are accustomed to using their nickname ("Johnnie"). Many of them like to make up a name, such as "Hotshot." Compare the motivational potential of the following responses with that given above: "Good work, Hotshot," or "Good work, Johnnie."

Be judicious. Do not address the student by name on every display lest the charm and motivation wear off quickly. If you wish to make humorous comments, be sure they will be viewed as such by the students and not taken as insults.

Report Student's Progress

There are several types of progress reports that students find motivating. In a set of practice questions, students like to know how many items they have completed and how many are left. Keep a tally for them on the display screen (Fig. 5.2).

Students frequently like to see a score of how well they are performing. In a drill the score can consist of a tally of number of items done and number of items done correctly. The number of items done wrong need not be displayed. This suggestion is made because the display of number of items done wrong may be very abrasive to immature students or those lacking in self-confidence. In one case, grade-school children were very upset when the lesson displayed the number of problems they had done wrong. In fact, some children asserted that the computer was wrong and others said it was broken! Some of them insisted on starting the exercise over again from the beginning in order to erase the display of the number of problems they had done wrong. The lesson was revised to display the number of problems they had attempted and the number they had done correctly. In that way the teacher could quickly figure out how well the child was doing, and the child was not embarrassed by the obvious display of number wrong.

Sometimes getting a good score or successfully completely a lesson is rewarding and motivating in and of itself. Sometimes students like an extra

USING PARENTHESES

Type the value of each expression:

$$(3 \times 4) + 2 =$$

FIG. 5.2   A tally of progress is often
motivating to the student.   *2 done*   *3 to go*

pat on the back. For example, seven-year-olds liked the display of a ribbon on the screen for good work. Many of them asked for a ribbon to take home to show their parents, and the teachers made paper copies of the displays of ribbons to send home with the children. Some students like the option of taking a self-test to see how well they are doing.

Add Variety

Employ a variety of instructional techniques. Students may become very bored if a single question-answer format is used throughout an entire lesson. A variety of formats may not only serve to gain the students' attention; it might also result in greater involvement and save time. In one CAI program students studied under one of four instructional conditions, three of which were the same fixed sequence of events (such as rule-examples-practice), and one of which was a random sequence of events. In the random sequence, content was randomly chosen from among the three fixed sequence strategies. A student might learn one concept in examples-rule-practice order and the next concept in practice-examples-rule order. No one instructional sequence was better than another, but students in the random sequence performed better and took less time than students in the fixed sequences.

Motivation is an important part of instruction. Anybody who works with computers cannot help but become fascinated with their graphic and/or musical capabilities. The tendency is to present elaborate graphics, animations, and musical sounds to motivate the student. Often simpler graphics or other motivational devices will serve equally well. In fact, students may not consider such elaborate effects motivating after their first exposure. Maintain perspective on the motivating effects of the "fun" things.

SELF-CONCEPT AND ANXIETY

Individualization and Academic Self-Concept

Can individualization result in affective as well as cognitive enhancement? If students work at their own level of understanding in CAI, they should attain a reasonable amount of success. Will this success be beneficial to their self-esteem? Since some students rarely succeed in the traditional environment, CAI can perhaps provide an opportunity for those students to experience success. On the other hand, one can speculate that the overall impact of CAI on academic self-esteem will be minimal, considered against the background of 10 or more years of low achievement in a basically nonsupportive environment. CAI probably offers its strongest potential for affecting academic self-concept positively in the early elementary-school years. We would like to believe that the proliferation of computers in schools will be accompanied by high quality lessons and that CAI will play a major role in raising the self-esteem of many students.

We do see students of all academic levels coming to school early and staying late for the privilege of working on computers, not only to program them but even to do mundane lessons like long division. The potential is certainly there.

Anxiety

Intuition and experience tell us that anxiety affects learning as well as performance on tests, that many of us are particularly anxious when studying certain subjects or when in the presence of certain individuals. Most people have at one time or another experienced the thumping heart when about to take a test; many have experienced personality clashes with classmates or teachers and noticed its impact on learning. CAI seems to be an instructional medium that can reduce student anxiety, and thus facilitate learning.

Researchers have attempted to reduce state anxiety in CAI by controlling instructional design variables. They have not been able to demonstrate that specific design procedures (e.g., statement of objectives, sequence of topics, response mode) reduce state anxiety. Furthermore, there is insufficient evidence to support the premise that low anxiety is desirable for good performance and high anxiety detrimental. For the present, disregard anxiety as a factor in the CAI lesson.

PROGRAM AND EVALUATE

After making human factors and management plans, leave the band of circles in the Ripple Plan to program, evaluate, and revise the unit. Plan revisions needed as determined by the preceding evaluation. Decide which aspects of instruction to put under computer control and what data to add to implement the management. Plan additions to smooth human-machine interaction and to motivate the learners.

Program the additions and revisions, test the lesson, and get somebody else to do so, too. Observe whether your revisions have actually remedied the problems noted earlier. Check to see if the management program is functioning as intended, and if learner-computer interaction is functioning smoothly. If the person who tests the unit experiences some difficulty meeting the criteria, consider several possible reasons. The instruction may be ambiguous, misleading, or insufficient. Perhaps the questions are poorly formulated. Perhaps you set unreasonable criteria. Discuss the unit with the student and with colleagues or others who might provide insights. Revise the unit accordingly.

SAMPLE LESSON

Let us continue with the sample lesson on engineering calculations at the third circle of the Ripple Plan. First, plan the revisions deemed necessary during the previous lesson tryout.

The learners did not know how to enter exponents (superscripts). Write a short sequence to step the learner through the procedure (Fig. 5.3). In addition add the following message to the bottom of every display where it is appropriate:

For exponent: Press Control-U, then digit.

The unit under development will be easy for the target population. If they answer a question wrong, the only feedback they need is the correct answer and a statement of why it is correct. Therefore, there is no need to allow for more than one try to get the correct answer.

The computer will control the flow of instruction within this unit because mastery here is essential to understanding succeeding concepts.

The criterion for mastery of each concept in the unit is three successive first ok's. Add a data-keeping mechanism to record the number of successive first ok's for each concept. In order to have enough questions to bring learners to criterion, generate a pool of 10 questions for each of Displays 3, 4, 5, and 7. The students will probably not find it difficult to meet this criterion, so at this time it is not necessary to generate review or remediation.

Write the computer program to include all of the above, and test the lesson. Then ask one or two others to do likewise. Make notes of problems and revise accordingly.

How to Enter Exponents

To get the computer to display a number as an exponent, press Control-U and then press the number.

Example:
To type cm^3, type   cm
           press   Control-U
           type   3

Now you do it. Type cm^3.

FIG. 5.3   Instructions to step student through a nonstandard procedure for entering a response.

OTHER UNITS OF INSTRUCTION

The rest of the units of instruction are generated in the same manner, following the Ripple Plan. Develop one aspect of instruction at a time; interact with others frequently; evaluate and revise. When all units of instruction are finished, return to the lesson level to complete the lesson.

6 Displays and Overall Lesson Structure

Now that the units of instruction have been generated, you are ready to focus on the overall lesson. First, evaluate and revise the design of the displays. Then complete the overall lesson.

Many of the suggestions given below will seem like nothing more than common sense and you will wonder why they are even mentioned. The reason is that such "common" sense is not commonly displayed in an unbelievable proportion of CAI lessons. This fact is true of lessons for large computer systems, as well as microcomputers, and of large commercially produced programs as well as those produced by individual authors. Many CAI authors ignore these apparently obvious principles when designing CAI lessons.

DISPLAYS

Draw Attention to Messages

In addition to generating the instruction in CAI, you have to design the layout of the display. By designing a display appropriately, the author can increase the probability that a student will pay particular attention to a message. Do not assume that if a message is presented the students will automatically notice it. The author must arrange the display so that they will. For example, when giving directions for proceeding to the next display, set directions apart from the rest of the content with a line or with plenty of space around them. When directions are embedded in other information at the bottom of a display (Fig. 6.1), students are not likely to notice them and

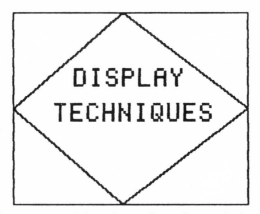

FIG. 6.1   Learners are not apt to notice directions that are embedded in other information.

will sit there staring at the display trying to figure out what to do. Similarly, if you want learners to pay special attention to one part of the presentation, design the display to do so.

Most people cannot attend to more than one thing at the same time. It is unreasonable to expect students to notice several things simultaneously. If a fair amount of text is followed immediately by an animation, students may still be reading the text while the animation is going on and not even notice it. First display the text. Then tell the learner to press a particular key when he is ready to see the animation.

Techniques.   To get students to pay extra attention to a particular part of the display, present that part differently from the rest. For example, use a different color for the starting point than for the rest of the display, or use color only for the starting point and white for the rest. If your computer system does not support color, use inverse, back on white (green), for the beginning and the normal white (or green) on black for the rest of the display, or use a different style or type size for the beginning. If your computer system does not provide for alternate sizes or characters, use some other form of contrast, such as extra s p a c e s between the letters or all CAPITAL LETTERS. Enclose the special material in a box, or underline it, or surround it with asterisks or other nonstandard characters. The idea is to attract attention by making a visually obvious distinction beween the part to be emphasized and the rest of the display.

Flashing is another method of drawing attention to some part of a display. The problem with flashing is deciding how long the flashing should last. Done too quickly, the student might not even notice it. Done over too long a period of time, the student will get bored. Some people find flashing to be physically disturbing.

Be careful not to overdo attention-getting techniques. If several parts of the display are in color, none of them will be distinctive. If many sections are framed with boxes or are underlined, none will seem more important then the others (Fig. 6.2).

Get Students to View Entire Display

The design of the visual display can dramatically affect the sequence in which students scan it. The visuals can be designed to indicate where a student should look first and how she should move her eyes across the display screen.

The starting point.   Get the student started in the right place by guiding the eye to the starting point. This can be accomplished in two ways. (1) Present only the material that must be noticed first, and nothing more, until the student requests more display by pressing a prespecified key. (2) Present all of the material at one time but make the starting point special in some way. Apply attention-getting techniques to draw the student's eye to the starting point.

Flow across the display.   The visual design can also control the rhythm of the flow across the page. Present the material in the order you want learners to notice it. The usual way of reading displays in English is from top to bottom and from left to right, so that once learners' eyes are at the bottom of a display they are not likely to look back up to the top or the middle.

Avoid minute changes.   When learners finish a display, they expect to continue on to the next one. The lesson author who wants them to look at

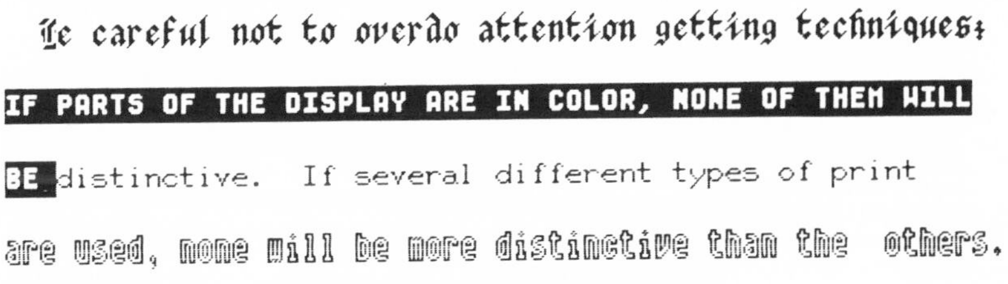

Be careful not to overdo attention getting techniques:

IF PARTS OF THE DISPLAY ARE IN COLOR, NONE OF THEM WILL

BE distinctive.   If several different types of print

are used, none will be more distinctive than the others.

FIG. 6.2   Conflicting attention getters.

an upper part of the display again, rather than continue to a new one, is violating the learners' expectation. Therefore, the author is obliged to apprise the learners explicitly of this change. Write a message to "Look above" or draw a line to direct attention.

A small change in just part of the text is also apt to go unobserved by the learners, particularly if it occurs in an unexpected place. Compare Fig. 6.3a and Fig. 6.3b. After responding to the question in Fig. 6.3a, a student will not necessarily look at the question again even though the heading mentions a "few questions." If he does read the question again, it might take him a minute or so to realize that there is a slight change. This combination of a change in an unexpected part of the display and the minuteness of the change, just two letters, make it highly unlikely that the student will be aware that a new question is being asked. Figure 6.4 shows a better way to make the new questions obvious. The format as well as the directions indicates to the student where to expect new questions.

Position response instructions and feedback. Experience has shown that in CAI students stop reading at the point where they encounter a cursor or an arrow indicating they are to make a response. Therefore, instructions about how to answer the question should be displayed before the student encounters this marker (Fig. 6.5); instructions presented after the marker are simply not read (Fig. 6.6).

Place feedback to the student's response near the response. If the response is at the top of the page, for example, and the feedback is in the middle or at the bottom, the student is not likely to notice it (Fig. 6.7). If the location of the response is in the middle of a body of text or other information, it will be difficult for the author to place the feedback near the response. In this case, use an attention-getting technique to draw the student's attention to the feedback, a device as simple as a line with an arrow pointing to the feedback.

Most students are not professional typists. When entering a response, they usually bend their heads over the keyboard and, for the most part, do not look up to see what is happening on the display until they have finished the response. Feedback must, therefore, be allowed to remain on the display until the student indicates he has had a chance to see it.

Display Design as a Learning Aid

It is sometimes possible to arrange the material on the display in a way that helps the learner understand and remember it. For example, if the student is to remember a list of items, present them as a list rather than in paragraph form. Compare the directions in Fig. 6.8 and Fig. 6.9.

a
Here are a few questions for you.

What is the distance between C and D?
Type in the word whole or half.
  ⧽

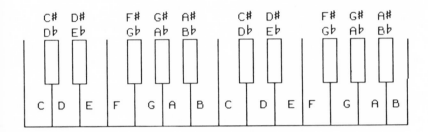

b
Here are a few questions for you.

What is the distance between D and E♭?
Type in the word whole or half.
  ⧽

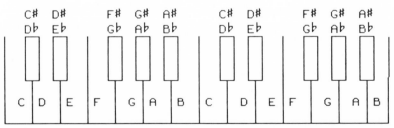

FIGS. 6.3a, 6.3b Minor changes in the display are likely to go unnoticed. (From computer-assisted instruction lesson, *Introduction to Scales*. Copyright © 1976 by Control Data Corporation. Reprinted by permission.)

Type in the word whole or half to
tell the distance between each pair
of notes.

1. C and D   > >   whole   ok
2. D and E   > >

FIG. 6.4   An alternative format for
Figs. 6.3a and 6.3b.

Table of Contents

Choose the topic you wish to
study. Type 1, 2, 3, or 4. >

1. The sounds of g.
2. The sounds of c.
3. The sounds of y.
4. The sounds of s.

FIG. 6.5   Directions about how to respond should precede the response
marker (>).

Table of Contents

Choose the topic you wish to
study. >

1. The sounds of g.
2. The sounds of c.
3. The sounds of y.
4. The sounds of s.

Type 1, 2, 3, or 4.

FIG. 6.6   Learner is not likely to
notice directions about how to
respond if they are placed after the response marker (>).

Learners find it easier to comprehend text if each line contains a meaningful component. It is not the length of the line that is critical to comprehension so much as whether the line represents a meaningful segment of
information.

Present only as much information at one time as you can expect the student to process or remember. One way to do so is to present a small amount
on each display. In some instances this is not satisfactory because the student must ultimately be able to look at the entire presentation, in order to
integrate the parts into a larger whole. If such is the case, present the concepts one at a time, instructing the student to press a particular key when
ready to go on to the next concept.

Display Techniques

CARDINAL PRINCIPLE: Keep the display uncluttered. The lesson should
be displayed so as to facilitate learning and not to impede it in any way.

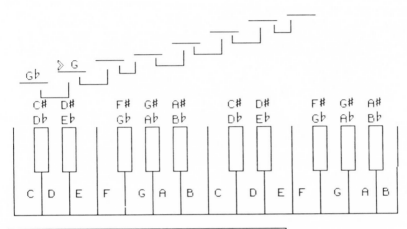

make a ⟦MAJOR⟧ scale

Start on low G♭ and
End on high G♭

wrong

If you want a short review, press HELP
To review the directions, press BACK
If you want to exit, press SHIFT-STOP

FIG. 6.7   Feedback should be placed near student's response. (From computer-assisted instruction lesson, *Introduction to Scales*. Copyright © 1976 by Control Data Corporation. Reprinted by permission.)

How to Enter Exponents

To get the computer to display a number as an exponent, press Control-U and then press the number.

Example:

To type cm³,   type   cm
                press   Control-U
                type   3

Now you do it. Type cm³.

FIG. 6.8   A list format may help the learner remember a list of directions.

How to Enter Exponents

To get the computer to display a number as an exponent, press Control-U and then press the number. For example, to type cm^3 type cm, then press Control-U, then type 3.

Now you do it. Type cm^3.

FIG. 6.9   Paragraph format of directions in Fig. 6.8.

Leave plenty of space between and around parts of the display (Fig. 6.10). CAI is unlike a textbook, where the publisher must keep the amount of empty space, and hence the number of pages to be printed, to a minimum.

Text.   A solid paragraph of text that is easy to read on paper may be tiring on the CAI display screen. Make the text as easy to read as possible, visually as well as content-wise. Use both uppercase and lowercase letters. People are accustomed to reading English text that uses both, so text should be presented this way in CAI. Obviously, it is possible to read text presented in uppercase only, but it is not as natural to the reader. Text is also difficult to read if it is crowded. If the display on your computer system crowds text when it is shown on every line, display it on every other line or allow a space and a half between lines. Allow for margins at top and bottom if possible, and at the sides as well. Ordinarily, text should be centered unless there is some special reason for not doing so.

Fidelity.   Sometimes, it is useful to present text in larger than standard size, particularly in lessons for small children. Two factors should be evaluated in making decisions about sized text, time required to plot the larger text, and fidelity of the enlarged characters. Students find it very boring to wait for the machine to display a word slowly when the letters are presented in large size. There may be situations in which the author wants to do so for emphasis, but for the most part, text to be read should be displayed as quickly as possible. In addition, the enlarged characters should not be distortions. Consider, for example, the shape of the letter *D* in Fig. 6.11. The lesson is obviously intended for a child who is just learning to read, yet the letter as presented is a very poor example because it does not reflect the true characteristics. Thus it is unacceptable for a beginning reader.

Timing.   Allow the learners to decide when to change displays. There is nothing more frustrating to learners than having something "wiped off" the

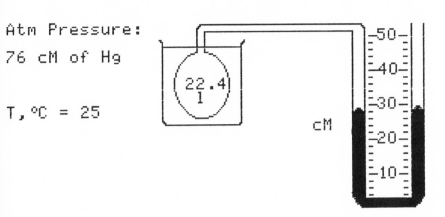

```
Atm Pressure:
76 cM of Hg


T, °C = 25
```

22.4
1

cM

-50-
-40-
-30-
-20-
-10-

```
PRESS:    H to heat
          C to cool
          RETURN to record data
```

FIG. 6.10 Uncluttered displays facilitate learning. (From computer-assisted instruction lessons, *Introduction to Inorganic Chemistry*. Copyright © 1982 by Stanley Smith. Reprinted by permission.)

```
D IS FOR DOG.
```

FIG. 6.11 The letter *D* lacks fidelity.

screen before they are finished studying it. The frustration is intensified when part of the text is overwritten by different text. Overwriting of this sort leaves students with the feeling that they do not know what is going on.

Avoid scrolling.   A computer display is said to scroll when the following situation occurs. The display is completely filled and there is no more room at the bottom; to make room for another line of text, each current line moves up one line, the top line simply disappears off the display screen, and the new line of text is displayed at the bottom. This moving up of the text is repeated as each additional line is displayed at the bottom. The effect is that of a sheet of paper being scrolled upward. It is not pleasing to the eye. More important, though, is that scrolling results in the loss of previous information that the student may wish to refer to. In some instances, students' incorrect answers may be scrolled off. They can't learn from their previous errors if the errors are not there to be studied. To avoid scrolling, erase those parts of the display that are no longer needed and replace with new text.

Graphics.   Keep diagrams as free of irrelevant details as possible. The student should be able to see what is critical to the concept being taught. Cluttered diagrams are not effective teaching presentations.

Overkill, using elaborate tables of data, is a common flaw in CAI lessons. Some authors generate elaborate tables but make little use of them. They may ask one question and then move on to an entirely new display. It is not necessary to generate and display a large amount of data just because the computer is capable of doing so. Generate tables only if the student is supposed to learn how to use a table of data or needs data in order to make inferences from it. When helping the student learn how to use the table, point to particular parts of the table that he should notice. When the student has finished attending to a particular section, erase the attention-getting graphics before continuing on to emphasize the next part of the table.

Poorly designed graphics may get in the way of learning. In Fig. 6.7, for example, the author intended to help the student by relating the names of the keys in the scale to their positions on the keyboard. Unfortunately, the display was poorly designed, and the responses do not synchronize with the keyboard. The result is needlessly confusing.

Sometimes, it takes a few seconds to display a complicated diagram or a picture composed of several characters. If such is the case, and the same diagram is to be used for several topics or a number of questions, draw the diagram just once. Simply present additional information or questions, rather than presenting entirely new displays. Time consumed by the replotting of the diagram may be frustrating to the student. Be sure to make it clear to the student that additional material is being added.

In CAI the author must be careful not to display too many things at one time, each demanding the student's attention. For example, a flashing message in more than one part of the display, or animation presented simultaneously with text elsewhere, becomes just too much for a person to attend to.

Color.   Color is attractive. A book that contains colored pictures is more appealing than one in black and white. A colored figure, such as a bird, is more attractive as feedback than a black and white one. Color may be attractive and hence motivating, but the color itself does not necessarily improve learning.

Color can be used for emphasis and can lead the eye to the starting place on a display. Sometimes, color is useful to help the student discriminate between two items. If color is an important aspect of a concept, use the name of the color in the message, in addition to displaying the item in color. Obviously, the color you describe should be the one you show. If you are teaching the colors of highway signs, for example, and write that the STOP sign is red, display it in red and not violet or blue.

A few further words of caution about common misuses of color. Using different colors on different parts of the display can fragment the content being presented. Some colors do not show up well against each other and make the text difficult to read.

Animation.   Animation is exciting for the author to program, but before you decide on animation, consider whether it is really needed in order to demonstrate the content being presented. An excellent example of the use of animation is to demonstrate the relationship between the flow of fluid and the opening and closing of valves.

One of the factors to consider in animation is timing. The animation should be fast enought to get the idea across without taking an excessive amount of time to be displayed. On the other hand, it should not go so fast that the student does not see what is happening. In some cases it might be useful to allow the student to slow down or speed up the animation.

Simulating animation.   It is sometimes possible to get the effect of animation without any actual animation. For example, to simulate a hopping frog, draw the frog, wait a second or two, erase the frog, draw an arc from the initial location of the frog to the place it is supposed to land, erase the arc, and redraw the frog. Computer systems vary in the speed with which figures can be displayed and erased, and in their capability of erasing just selected parts of the screen. The particular technique for animation that the author selects will obviously vary with the system. The point to remember is that you should not feel constrained by the apparent limits of the system. By clever programming, or by conferring with the programmer and explaining exactly what you want the program to do, you can frequently get the system to do more than appears possible on the surface.

OVERALL LESSON STRUCTURE

After generating all of the individual units, put them together into a cohesive whole. Make management and human factors decisions for the overall lesson, add introductory and concluding displays, evaluate, revise, and document. A discussion of the first four topics follows. The last three (evaluation, revision, and documentation) are treated in the next chapter.

Management Decisions

Two aspects of lesson flow are managed at the lesson level: (1) rules for advancing from one unit to the next, and (2) the sequence, that is, the order in which the units will be studied. Before generating rules for the computer to manage instruction, decide where to assign control of management. Will you allow the learner to proceed from one unit to the next, regardless of performance in the unit? Will you assign control to the instructor or to the computer? Will you present an index and allow learners to decide which units they want to study and in which order, or will you place some, or all such decisions, under computer and/or instructor control?

Criteria for advancing.   Guidelines for decision making here are much the same as decision making for management within each unit of instruction and are related to those decisions. Decisions depend on the goal of the lesson, the role of the lesson in the curriculum, and the ability of the target students to manage their own learning in this lesson. If you have chosen computer management *within* units, chances are you should also choose computer management *between* units, and for the same reasons. Assign computer control if a standard of performance is part of the goal, or if the target learners are not good managers of learning in this subject. If the content is hierarchical in nature, and understanding one unit depends on the knowledge acquired in previous units, assign to the computer the control of conditions for advancing from one unit to the next.

If you do assign the computer control over progress from one unit to the next, you can base management decisions on students' performance within the unit or on a quiz at the end. For example, program the computer to advance students to the next unit of instruction if the proportion of first ok's is 75%. Alternatively, you can present a quiz at the end of the unit. If a student's performance meets a preset criterion, advance her; otherwise, review or remediate.

A performance level of 75% is *not* advocated for all lessons. The criterion or performance level chosen depends on the purpose of the lesson. It can be set at 100% if perfection is part of the goal. However, not all lessons have the same goals. If the lesson is an introduction to a subject, to be followed by additional instruction, the goal may simply be that the learners gain a minimum level of understanding. The expectation is that they will improve their understanding in subsequent instruction. Since the CAI lesson is just an introduction, it is not necessary for them to perform at 100% on first ok's. Hence, a less stringent standard of performance is in order.

Decide whether to assign control of the sequence of instructional units to the computer or the student. Ordinarily, the subject matter determines the sequence of topics of instruction, so the computer advances the student from one topic to the next accordingly. There are times, however, when it is beneficial to allow the student to start at some point other than the beginning of the sequence or to change it. For example, if the lesson is too long to complete in the time allotted, the student will have to resume studying at another time and should be able to resume at the place he left at the previous session (not the first topic). The instructor may feel that a learner needs to review some selected topics but not all of them. Sometimes, learners want to review a topic to feel more confident about their knowledge. All of these are reasons for providing a table of contents and allowing either learner or instructor (or both) control over sequence. There are also arguments for not doing so.

If the lesson has a table of contents, and students are studying the lesson for the first time, you would expect them to begin with the first topic, particularly if it is labeled "Introduction." Unfortunately, poor learners have been observed to begin studying by choosing a topic in the middle of the table of contents. They are apparently not aware of the significance of the sequence, even if the display includes the message, "If this is your first time in the lesson, start with the introduction."

The decision to allow learner control of instruction depends on the ability of the target population to manage their own instruction. If they are sophisticated learners, and the lesson is supplementary drill or practice, allow them to choose topics to review if they wish to do so. If the goal of the lesson is to allow the learners self-study, allow them to select units in any order.

Some authors who allow learners control over the sequence of instruction add a display to the end of each unit telling the learner what options are available (Fig. 6.12).

It's a good idea to have a "default" condition in which the computer advances the learner from one unit to the next, even if the lesson does allow the instructor or learners the option of managing the instructional path.

This is the end of "Arithmetic operations."

Press Control-B if you want to review this topic.
Press ESC to return to the Table of Contents.
Press RETURN to go on to the next topic.

FIG. 6.12   Example of end-of-unit display.

Some learners will not care whether the option is available or not and will prefer not to bother with these decisions. For example, program the computer to move the learner from one unit to the next in a prespecified sequence but allow them to go back to the table of contents at any time.

Placement.   A pretest may be given at the beginning of the lesson to determine proper placement. Although the author has specified entry behaviors that are expected of all students, some of them may have some knowledge beyond the minimum. Such students can then be moved past concepts they happen to know already, but which you do not expect most students to know before studying this lesson.

Human Factors

Introduce special function keys.   Most keys display a letter or other character such as "?". When the student presses that key, the character appears on the screen. Some keys, called function keys, have a name, such as RETURN or NEXT or CONTROL. They do not display a character when pressed, but serve a special function, such as returning to the index, getting help, going back one display, and so on. Some authors present a full-screen display, which is a long list of these keys and their functions, at the beginning of the lesson. It is difficult for students to remember all of this information, particularly if they will not use all of it immediately. Introduce the use of the one or two special keys students will need to use immediately; introduce the others as they are needed in the lesson. The author can recommend that the classroom instructor or student type the list on a card and tape it to the terminal when using the lesson. Another alternative is to display a list of keys and their functions at the bottom of the display screen, if doing so does not clutter things too much. The list at the bottom of the display is particularly beneficial because it reminds students that certain options are available, as well as telling them how to access those options. In addition, information at the bottom of the display doesn't get lost or misplaced like cards taped to terminals.

Check for consistent use of keys.   Just as it is important to be consistent in the use of keys within a unit, the same holds for an entire lesson or a series of lessons. Use the same key for the same purpose throughout a lesson, and throughout a series of lessons. For example, always use the same key (like ENTER or RETURN or NEXT) to initiate answer judging or to go on to the next display.

Other aids.   If the lesson is a complex inquiry or simulation, provide students with adequate information about how to get around, perhaps even providing diagrams so that they know where they are and how to get where they want to go next. A *User's Manual* may be needed to accompany such a lesson.

Jargon or unexplained terms.   If it takes a moment to transfer the lesson from the disk, say something like, "One moment, please" or "We are preparing the lesson." Avoid a statement like "Loading characters," because the student is not likely to understand the word *loading* in this context.

Introductory Displays

Title page.   The first display, as in a book, is the title page. It includes the name of the lesson, the name of the author(s), the institutional affiliation, and the year it was written or most recently revised, and copyright information. If the lesson was produced by more than one person, say a lesson designer and a programmer, list the names and responsibilities of each. Animation of fancy artwork on the title page is attractive the first time the student enters the lesson. After the first time, the novelty wears off and the students become impatient waiting for the computer to quit doing the artwork and get on with the lesson. Some authors present graphics on the title page, but allow the learner to abort the graphics and proceed to the lesson if she so chooses.

Purpose or objectives.   A short statement of purpose helps orient the students and tells them what to expect. Stating objectives snares attention and directs students to the material to be learned and away from other material. Be brief and precise. Students like to get on with the lesson and become impatient with lengthy statements at the beginning.

Instructions or rules.   Sometimes a single set of instructions or rules applies to an overall lesson and is not written specifically for one unit of instruction. The guidelines presented above for designing a single unit are also applicable to the overall lesson. Present the rules one at a time, allow the learner to try them out before using them in the lesson, and ask appropriate questions to be sure the learner understands them.

Table of contents.   A table of contents, sometimes called a menu or index, can serve a number of functions. It enables learners to resume instruction where they previously left off if they were unable to complete the work earlier. It enables learners to find and review those sections where they feel they need extra practice. Instructors can use the table of contents to get an overview of what is in the lesson and to override computer control.

If you provide a table of contents and allow students to choose which units to do, mark the units they have already completed (Fig. 6.13). Students sometimes forget the content of each item in the table of contents and don't remember whether they did it or not. Marking completed topics prevents their wasting time getting into sections they have already done (unless they want to review). The markings will also remind them of sections that still need to be studied and may prevent their skipping parts that they thought they had already done.

If you decide to allow the learner some options in a table of contents, do not provide too many. A succession of choices or one subindex after another becomes confusing. Even if the students are not bewildered by all of the choices, they may only choose or make use of one or two of the alternatives. In one CAI lesson, for example, the authors allowed the students to choose any one of 16 instructional strategies. For the most part, only 3 of those 16 strategies were ever picked by students.

Additional information.   Certain lessons require extensive directions, as in games or simulations. These are lessons that learners are apt to repeat many times. Since they do not need to read the instructions every time, it is useful to add a display that allows them the choice of reading or skipping the rules.

If additional equipment is needed, such as an audio device or light pen or workbook, present this information on a separate display.

Two additional kinds of information are often provided only in the documentation that accompanies a lesson, like a brochure or teacher's manual. These state the prerequisites and also the target population. If this information is pretty much what is expected, it is not essential that it be repeated in the introduction to the lesson. For example, if the subject matter is addition

---

TABLE OF CONTENTS

Type the number of the topic you wish to do.
    *Indicates topics completed.
    *1. Introduction
    2. Logical IF
    3. Arithmetic IF
    4. Logical operators

FIG. 6.13 Table of contents showing topics student has completed.

of fractions for upper-elementary students, the prerequisites are standard across most curricula and commonly known. If, on the other hand, the lesson is designed as part of a specific program, such as a Red Cross course in first aid, or to accompany a particular textbook, this information should be conveyed in one of the introductory displays. In addition, if the lesson is designed for a specific target population, such as hard-of-hearing people, this information should also be presented in an introductory display.

Concluding Displays

Students like to know how well they have performed in the lesson. They also like to know how they stand relative to the rest of the class. This information can be presented as one of the concluding displays. If appropriate, you can also keep a record of the top performers in a lesson and list them in a "Hall of Fame." The Hall of Fame can be displayed at the end of the lesson to show learners how they compare to the "experts."

Students like to know when they have reached the end of the lesson. They know how to tell when they are at the end of a book, but they have no way of knowing that they are at the end of a CAI lesson unless you tell them. Add a concluding display that conveys this information.

Tell the students what options are now available, and how to access them, as suggested for the end of a topic (Fig. 6.12).

To summarize, make decisions and plans for management, human factors, and initial and concluding displays. Add them to the lesson; that is, write the computer program. The completed lesson begins with a title page and is followed by introductory displays, the units of instruction, and concluding displays. Now the lesson is ready for the final components of development: evaluation and revision of the entire lesson.

7 Evaluation

After all of the components of the lesson have been generated, it is time to evaluate and revise the lesson as a whole. Lesson evaluation includes revising the measures of student performance generated during initial planning, doing formative and summative evaluations, making plans for lesson maintenance, and writing the documentation.

Evaluation is an integral part of lesson development, from initial planning through lesson completion. During initial planning the author generates tentative, sometimes incomplete measures to evaluate each student's performance. Then, when creating the instruction, each component of each unit is evaluated, in order to improve both the instruction and the interaction. In completing the lesson, evaluation serves two additional purposes: (1) to review and revise the student performance measures that were generated during initial planning, and (2) to evaluate the overall lesson. Incomplete sets of performance measures are expanded or revised. Completed sets are reviewed for consistency with the lesson. By now gross errors within units will have been corrected, but other minor ones may remain. Although the units were evaluated as part of the Ripple Plan, the lesson as a whole must also be evaluated to determine whether learners can move smoothly from one unit to the other, and whether the total lesson achieves the goals set for the learners. Finally, documentation is provided for users, and a mechanism for lesson maintenance is arranged.

Formal evaluation of the entire lesson takes on added significance for lessons prepared for stand-alone microcomputer systems. CAI systems that run on one large central computer have the advantage, in that just one copy of the lesson is used by all students. Although it is bad procedure to present a lesson before it has been thoroughly and systematically evaluated, only one copy needs to be revised if the lesson does happen to contain errors. After the author corrects the errors, all students will then study this revised version.

The situation is quite different for microcomputer systems, that is, stand-alone computers that operate from disks or cassettes. Hundreds and thousands of copies, not just one copy of the lesson, are used by students. If a lesson contains errors, they must either be corrected on every disk or cassette, or else new, revised disks must be distributed. It may be impossible to know who all the users are, if the lesson is widely used. Even if one could reach all holders of erroneous lessons, the cost would be prohibitive. Therefore, it is particularly important that evaluation be carefully planned and implemented if lessons are written for microcomputer systems.

EVALUATION MEASURES

Measure the Student's Performance

Review initial set of measures.   The goal here is to complete tentative measures for evaluating each student's performance, or to revise completed measures, in order to make them consistent with the lesson as it finally evolves. Evaluate your plans for measuring student performance. Did you complete the measures during initial planning? If so, review them now to see if they measure goal achievement adequately. It may be necessary to generate some new items and to delete others. For example, if you added instruction that you had not planned initially, generate questions to test understanding of those concepts. Perhaps you shortened or changed the lesson in some way; in that case, some of the initial items may no longer be appropriate and should be deleted.

Complete tentative measures.   If the initial measures were only prototype or tentative items, they should now be expanded and completed. If you plan an end-of-the-lesson quiz, use the goals of the lesson and of the individual units as a guide for generating questions. Perhaps the lesson is a simulation. Some new performance measures may now become evident that were not at all apparent during initial planning. For example, in a simulation of patient care, the tentative measure of student performance was simply completing the lesson, that is, managing the patient without making a fatal error. Now that the lesson is ready, you see that it is also possible to measure the quality of care by the kinds of decisions the student makes: the number that are good and those that are poor but nonfatal. Another measure of performance might be the time the student requires to make these decisions.

Check validity.   Content validity is as important in CAI as in other forms of instruction. A test is valid if it measures whether the student has achieved the goals of the lesson. The test should not be a measure of other skills. Suppose the goal is to identify the notes on the musical scale. An example of a valid question is one that displays a note on the scale and asks the student to name it. An invalid question, for the given goal, is one that asks the student to identify the beat, such as quarter note. An additional kind of validity requires attention in CAI: knowing how to enter responses and being able to do so easily. A valid test should not require the student to figure out the form the answer should take, nor should it require him to be a good typist, for example, unless that is the goal of the lesson.

Measure Lesson Effectiveness

Pretest-posttest.   In addition to measuring students' performance, some authors like to determine the extent to which performance can be attributed to the lesson. A test at the end of the lesson, called a posttest, measures the learner's knowledge after he has completed the lesson. However, a posttest alone does not tell how much of the performance is attributable to the CAI lesson and how much to knowledge acquired elsewhere. One way to obtain this information is to generate a pretest, too. If the student does the pretest, the lesson, and the posttest all in one session, the difference between the scores will be a measure of the lesson's effectiveness. Unfortunately, there are also drawbacks to giving a pretest. First, it takes time. In addition, since most students do not know the subject matter content, they feel that trying to answer the questions is a waste of time. It may also be disconcerting for the student to be unable to answer one question after another and may discourage his use of the lesson altogether.

How, then, to resolve the dilemma? Consider the target population and the content of the lesson. If you expect some members of the target population to know some of the topics in the lesson, provide a pretest. You will then be able to determine which part of the posttest results to ascribe to the lesson. If an item is answered correctly on both pretest and posttest, performance can be attributed to knowledge gained elsewhere. If the student fails an item on the pretest but passes it on the posttest, performance can be attributed to the lesson.

When the CAI lesson is intended as the initial or primary source of instruction, a posttest will probably be sufficient to measure achievement attributable to the lesson. The assumption is that most of the target learners will have about the same entry level knowledge. This assumption can be tested during student trials.

Current research in adaptive testing provides promise that, in the future, it may be possible to program the computer to determine the student's knowledge based on a minimum number of questions. Rather than present the same predetermined number of questions to each student, questions will be generated as required to probe each one's level of understanding. Thus, if a learner responds correctly to an initial set of questions, the computer will generate additional questions to determine the depth of understanding. Conversely, if the learner's initial responses are incorrect, the computer will probe to diagnose the source of the difficulty, but the student will not be obliged to answer questions beyond his level of understanding.

Questionnaire.   An opinion questionnaire can be attached to the end of a CAI lesson to obtain students' attitudes about the lesson. Students are most likely to take time to respond to the questionnaire if it is short and easy to take. The items should clearly distinguish between opinions related to the medium (the use of CAI) and those related to the instruction (subject matter). Some examples follow.

Choose your response. Type its number.

The lesson helped me learn the subject matter content.

1. Strongly agree.
2. Agree.
3. No opinion either way.
4. Disagree.
5. Strongly disagree.

What do you see as the most important advantage of doing this lesson on the computer?

1. Learn more in the same amount of time.
2. Learn the same amount of material in less time.
3. Learn with less difficulty.
4. Better understanding of the material.
5. None — CAI has no particular advantage.

Completion rate.   In CAI you can keep a record of the number of students who complete a lesson. Although the fact that all students complete a lesson is no guarantee that it is effective, the fact that a large proportion do not complete it is evidence that something is wrong. If the students testing the lesson are representative of the target population and serious about their studies, a high dropout rate is a strong warning that the lesson should be revised.

Proportion correct on first try.   The proportion of first ok's provides an estimate of how well the student is learning the material. A student should be able to progress through a tutorial lesson at a reasonable performance level, say 75%. As will be shown later, lessons are revised until most students achieve a minimum criterion of this kind. This criterion relates to performance *while* the student is studying the lesson and should not be confused with performance *after* the lesson has been completed. When a student is in the act of studying a lesson, one should not expect as high a mastery level as after the lesson is completed. A record of percentage of first ok's will also be useful later, when the lesson is completed and in use. These data enable the instructor to identify those students who are having difficulty with a particular section. If an entire class is performing at a level below that which is expected, the instructor will know that the lesson is not effective for this group of students.

Time.   The time required for each unit of instruction can serve as an indicator of units that are particularly difficult or time-consuming. Total time in the lesson is also important because students and instructors must usually fit CAI instruction into an overall schedule.

FORMATIVE EVALUATION

Definitions

Operational readiness.   A lesson is said to be operationally ready when it is usable by an entire class. There are three criteria for operational readiness:

1. The content is accurate.
2. The lesson is sufficiently agreeable to the students, so that they are willing to complete it.
3. The target students can do the lesson without a monitor's presence.

Formative evaluation.   Evaluation that brings a lesson to operational readiness is called formative evaluation. Since the first draft of every lesson is just that, a *first* draft, it should be subjected to reviews by experts as well as by student trials and then revised as needed. If major revisions are necessary after the first tryout, additional tryouts should be conducted. The end product of this process is a lesson that is operationally ready.

Purpose

Formative evaluation increases the probability that the lesson will be revised as needed. It has been found that if evaluation takes place only after the lesson has been completed, most authors resist any major changes or revisions. The result may be a poor or even unusable lesson.

The model for formative evaluation is presented in Figure 7.1. The components are a compilation of recommendations of many successfully published CAI lesson authors. Most models of formative evaluation include the same major components but differ in the number of passes, the temporal position in the procedure in which student interviews are held, and the criterion set for operational readiness.

The model anticipates the need for more than one tryout. Experienced instructional designers in both traditional media and CAI admonish that the best lessons are those that have gone through more than one revision. Even the best can be improved.

The purpose of each component in the model is discussed next, followed by suggestions for carrying out the procedures.

First Tryout: Components

Review by experts.   The first step in formative evaluation is a review by a subject matter expert. Obviously, the content of the lesson must be correct; content errors will have been corrected before this phase of lesson development because the individual units of instruction have undergone continuous tryouts and revisions as part of the Ripple Plan. Nevertheless, it is important to ask an expert to examine the lesson for content accuracy and for omissions. Doing so is particularly important if the lesson is designed by a small group that includes a subject matter expert, a programmer, and a lesson designer. When a lesson is generated by such a group, the subject matter expert is frequently not an active participant in all aspects of instructional development. Sometimes the lesson designer and the computer programmer inadvertently introduce content errors when making the transition from the subject matter expert's plan to writing the script and programming it.

Another type of expert reviewer is an instructor who has taught the subject matter to the target population, preferably someone who has functioned on a one-to-one basis with students. Such a reviewer can provide suggestions about pedagogical aspects, such as ways of improving the presentation or of providing feedback in one unit or another. It is probably too late at this point in the development to make major revisions in teaching techniques. However, even minor changes can often improve the lesson significantly.

Major revisions.   The distinction is made between major and minor revisions because it is inefficient to revise the computer program after every tryout by every individual. Major revisions are those that must be imple-

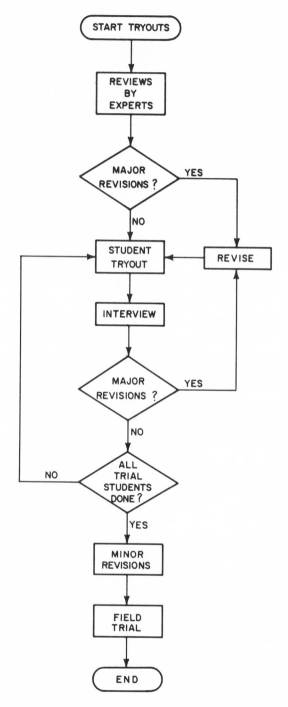

FIG. 7.1 Procedure for formative evaluation.

mented before the next person tries the lesson. For example, any content errors are major. There is no point in subjecting students to erroneous information even in student trials. Revisions that are strongly recommended by the instructor/reviewer are also major revisions. If the person doing the lesson comes to a dead end and cannot proceed, a major revision is required.

Minor revisions.   Typographical errors and minor changes in wording are errors that do not interfere with the lesson flow. Since they do not require immediate revision they are considered minor.

Tryouts by individual students.   A student tryout is done with one student at a time, to find technical flaws in the lesson (such as overwrites or branching to dead ends), deficiencies in the instruction, and time needed to complete the lesson. An additional goal is to assess students' attitudes toward the lesson. Finally, if the lesson includes a posttest, student tryouts help evaluate the validity of the test.

You might expect that with all of the reviewing and revising during the development of the instruction there would be no technical problems at this point. Remember, however, that the flow of the lesson has not been tested by students. Individual sections may work well, but when students test the entire lesson they may find themselves repeating a section over and over because of a programming error. They may press some unanticipated keys and find a dead end in the lesson. The process of revising during earlier trials may have resulted in creating new errors, such as accidental overwrites. (An overwrite occurs when two lines of text are displayed on top of each other on the same line in the display.)

Deficiencies in the instruction will vary. Some ambiguities in presentations and in questions may remain despite earlier revisions. The instruction may lack a sufficient number of examples, or the feedback may be inadequate. These shortcomings may not have been apparent in earlier revisions. Entire skills may have been omitted, and the need to teach them becomes apparent during the formative evaluation. For example, one experienced author of a CAI lesson reported a formative evaluation in which students functioning well in individual units of a lesson in signed number arithmetic did poorly in the final section, which consisted of mixed practice of addition, subtraction, and multiplication. The author found it necessary to add instruction to help students discriminate between problem types.

The time students need to complete lessons is particularly important in CAI because in many environments, such as secondary and postsecondary institutions, classes are scheduled for fixed lengths of time, say 50 minutes. CAI lessons must fit into these time limits. In elementary schools times are more flexible, but the instructor needs to know how much time to allow for students to complete CAI assignments. CAI must be integrated as to time as well as to content into the school day.

Student attitude must be sufficiently positive so that the student is not only willing to try the lesson, but also to complete it. If students find the lesson unacceptable, they will not complete it no matter how wonderful it seems to the lesson designer and the experts.

Tryouts are done individually in order to obtain information that is not contained in the quantitative computer-generated data, such as the number of correct responses or time taken. Students make spontaneous verbal comments expressing various emotions: they may turn to the observer and ask, "What do you mean here?"; they may take extensive notes on paper even though they know that the subject matter is covered in their textbooks. Students sometimes intentionally enter incorrect responses to see why those responses are wrong. Observing individual students allows such anomalies to be documented. This information subsequently helps the author interpret the data generated by the computer: the student spent an inordinate amount of time on a particular section because he was taking notes; or the performance was poor because the instruction was ambiguous.

Student tryouts are also helpful for validating the posttest. Students may perform at an acceptable level in the lesson but perform very badly on one or more items in the test. The author should investigate whether this performance is due to a faulty question or omissions in the instruction.

Student interviews.   The purpose of student interviews is to obtain suggestions for lesson improvement and to gain a deeper understanding of why certain parts of the instruction are difficult for the students. Students, even poor performers, can provide the designer with valuable insights. In one instance, for example, a remedial student in arithmetic did not understand the meaning of the expression *Sample,* which was meant to indicate that the following was an example of how to do a problem. The author explained the meaning to her and asked how she would phrase the information. The student suggested the sentence: "This is the way you're supposed to do it." How simple and how apt!

In the model presented here, the interview immediately follows each student tryout. You may choose to interview each student after completion of the lesson, or you may choose to interview the students as a group after everybody has completed it. The advantage of immediate interviews is that the student can discuss the lesson best while it is fresh in his memory. The advantage of group interviews is that students actuate each other during the course of discussion. A comment by one student may remind another of a point that concerned him, which he had forgotten to mention. Students may be more willing to talk about problems if they hear that other students also had problems with the lesson.

Field trial.   The purpose of the field trial is to check the revisions that were made after the individual trials and to locate and correct any remaining errors in the lesson. The trial enables the author to check on technical matters, such as data collection and student management routines, in a small group setting.

Field testing is carried out only once, and not on every tryout. The field testing is done after the lesson designer is satisfied that no further major revisions are required. If more than one tryout is necessary, postpone the field trial until after all tryouts with individual students are completed.

Second and Successive Tryouts

The purpose of the second and successive tryouts is to determine whether the revisions made after the first tryout have really improved the lesson. After the first tryout, it is assumed that no further check of content accuracy is needed. It may not be necessary to conduct further student interviews at this point or to test as many individuals in the second and later trials as in the first.

As an example of the value of further tryouts after major revisions, let us continue our discussion of the lesson on signed number arithmetic reported above. Remember that during formative evaluation the lesson author found it necessary to add a section of instruction to help students discriminate between problem types. At the same time, she reduced the number of examples in each instructional section. This change was made at the request of the classroom instructors, who felt that the additional instruction made the lessons too long. The lesson author then did a second tryout to evaluate the revisions. Results showed that students who performed at a level below 80% during instruction did worse than those who had performed at that level before the lesson was revised. Therefore, the examples were put back into the lesson, and performance improved on the third tryout.

Author Preparation

Before you begin, prepare to accept criticism and to keep an open mind about the kind of revisions recommended by experts and students. The purpose of these tryouts is not to be judgmental that the lesson is "good" or "bad." The purpose is to bring the lesson to operational readiness, to enable the students to accomplish the goal of the lesson. Consider the data that are collected and the comments of reviewers and students as constructive information, not as an assault on your creation. Weigh the data objectively before accepting or rejecting the criticism. Then make decisions about revision.

Data to Collect

During student tryouts collect two kinds of data: observational and computer-generated. If possible, use the CAI system to record as much of the information as possible. Have observers do what the computer cannot. Since they must identify the displays for which they write comments, observers need a quick and efficient way to identify these displays. One system that has been found satisfactory is to place an identifying code number at the top of each display. In the sample lesson on engineering operations, for example, the displays in the unit on arithmetic operations might be coded as ar1, ar2, and so on. If a student gives an unanticipated response on the second display, the observer can simply record the response and the display code, ar2.

What data should you collect? First, let us consider data that can be recorded by the computer. The suggestions following are made with respect to direct, tutorial instruction. Some of these recommendations would be meaningless in a discovery learning or drill lesson. Certain of the measures to be recommended for formative evaluation were recommended earlier for evaluation of students' performance, but the purpose is different here. In formative evaluation the measures provide a basis for revising the lesson *before* it is completed. In summative evaluation, the measures will evaluate the lesson in terms of student performance *after* the lesson is completed.

Most tutorial lessons are generated as units, according to the task analysis. Collect the data so as to analyze the results for each unit. Overall lesson data do not show which specific sections need revision.

Number of first ok's.   It is assumed that on some questions, at least, the student will be allowed a second or third try. If the student is unable to answer a "reasonable" proportion of the questions correctly on the first try, chances are the instruction is ambiguous, misleading, or insufficient. The criterion for an acceptable proportion of first ok's can be based on the overall performance of individual students on a section of instruction or on the performance of all students on a single question. Some authors judge a unit operational if students perform at 70% accuracy. Others base the decision to revise on the number of students who miss each question. If 40% of the students answer incorrectly, authors make major revisions on either the questions or the instructional material.

One experienced author has ascertained that if the proportion of first ok's is consistently low, students are having so much difficulty in understanding that the instruction requires improvement. The converse however, is not true; although a unit is difficult for the students, the proportion of first ok's may be satisfactory.

Time.   It was noted earlier that a measure of total time in a lesson is information that is needed for scheduling purposes. However, total time is insufficient information for lesson revision because it does not reveal how the time is spent. The student may repeat sections, spend most of her time on one section, complete the lesson, or leave it before finishing. Program the computer to gather this specific information. It is true that an observer can make a note of such events during individual student trials. However, later, when doing a trial with a group of students, the observer will not be able to keep track of this data for all of them.

Responses.   The author is not always able to anticipate every correct response students are apt to give. Unfortunately, unanticipated correct responses are judged wrong by the computer. If the computer keeps a record of all these responses, the author can identify such program shortcomings and correct them. For example, the authors of a CAI chemistry lesson asked students to type the symbol for the ion commonly formed by Cl. The computer's record of students' responses showed that many of them typed Cl^{-1}, an acceptable response. However, the computer had been programmed to accept only Cl^-. The response data enabled the lesson authors to revise the lesson to judge both responses correct.

Students sometimes give wrong answers that the lesson designer does not anticipate. If the data reveal that many students give the same incorrect answer, the author can add feedback specific to the error. It was suggested earlier that on the first draft of the lesson the author should neither try to anticipate all wrong answers nor write feedback for them. Nevertheless, your experience may have led you to anticipate certain incorrect responses and to write feedback for them on the first draft. Keep a record of the number of students who do, in fact, make these anticipated errors. If only a small proportion do so, the feedback should remain as corrective information for those who need it. If a large proportion of students make the same mistake and require corrective feedback, then the main body of instruction is inadequate. Revise it to prevent the misunderstanding from recurring.

If at all possible, provide a computer note file in which the student may type comments from any point in the lesson. The student may be more willing to write a comment than to make it in a face-to-face interview. Assurance of anonymity may increase the number and forthrightness of the comments. Sometimes the lesson author does not understand the thought processes behind a student's unanticipated but reasonable response. The computer will judge such an answer wrong because the author did not think of it. A comment from the student explaining his reasoning will enable the author to revise the lesson and accept this response in the future.

Requests for help.   The emphasis on writing a lean first draft results in the lesson providing few, if any, help sequences that the student can access on his own initiative. A record of the parts of instruction in which the student seeks help will tell you (1) if the "helps" you provide are actually used, and (2) where you should provide additional help. If the majority of students in the trials ask for help at a particular point, you probably need to revise that part of the instruction. If just a few students request help, design and make it available only to those who request it.

Observation.   Some data, such as spontaneous student behavior and unanticipated outcomes, cannot be obtained by the computer but must be generated by a human observer. Data to be gathered by the observer are discussed later under the section, "Student trials".

Procedures for Tryouts

Reviews by experts.   Orient the experts to the purpose of the review. Be sure they know the intended target population. It is preferable that reviews not be done long distance, but rather at the site of the development. Allow reviewers to do the lesson without interrupting to tell them what you had in mind at one point or another. If you have to do so, the lesson needs revision at that point. If your system supports a note file, suggest that reviewers use it as they go along. If a note file is not possible on your CAI system, provide paper for the reviewer to jot down notes. Before asking an expert to review the lesson, prepare a list of specific questions you would like to have answered. Were there any content errors? Which aspects of the pedagogy are particularly good or particularly poor? Does the reviewer have suggestions for improving the lesson? After the expert completes the review, ask for comments. If the comments are vague ("It looks ok") or incomplete, ask any questions on your list about which the reviewer has not commented. If the expert's review indicates that major revisions are warranted, make them now.

Student trials.   There is no fixed rule for the number of students who should participate in these tryouts; plan on about five or six. A sample of one is obviously insufficient. There are bound to be individual differences within a target population. If you select only one student, he may be more knowledgeable than the average or not as smart. Results of a single student tryout might thus distort the true picture of lesson effectiveness. A good rule of thumb is to quit doing individual tryouts when you feel you are no longer obtaining new information for revision.

The data are most likely to be reliable if you select students from the target population. If a lesson is intended for vocational students, test it with vocational students, not with professional students. Be sure to include some bright or above average students; they are most likely to speak up. The first version of a lesson usually has many faults. Average or below average students are not as likely to speak up, because they find it difficult to believe that deficiencies are the designer's fault if the lesson is hard, or impossible, to understand.

Before a trial begins, explain its purpose to the student. The student should understand that the lesson is in a raw state and needs to be polished. His job is to assist in that process. This role is different from the one usually assumed by the student, and you must communicate this difference to him. Such an explanation may prompt at least one or two of the poorer performers to contribute insightful comments.

To obtain the most reliable and complete information, the author should be present to observe the trials. It is sometimes difficult for other observers to transmit the exact nature of the trial; they may not fully appreciate the importance of certain actions that transpire and consequently may fail to document them.

Make notes about technical and mechanical errors that arise. There may be misspellings. A student may inadvertently press the wrong key and find herself in the wrong section. A display may be difficult to read because it contains too much information. A student may press the wrong key because she does not understand the directions. Make a note of displays at which students look puzzled or those in which they interpret the content differently from the way you intended.

DO NOT stop a student while he is doing the lesson to explain what you had in mind. Help the student ONLY if he is literally unable to proceed because of a programming error. If the directions, instruction, or questions are not understandable from the CAI lesson itself, that part of the presentation must be revised. The goal is to make the presentation clear to the student when no instructor is present. When you observe, you are present as a recorder of events; you are not present as an instructor.

Interview the student after he completes the lesson. Ask for his overall opinion about the lesson, and which parts he liked best and least. Ask for recommendations for changes. Ask specifically about items on which you took notes during the observation, if they have not already been discussed. For example, if the student seemed unsure about a presentation, ask him why he was unsure or how he interpreted it.

The interview will provide the greatest amount of constructive information for the lesson author if you tell students that their comments are needed to perfect the lesson. Conduct the interview in a nonthreatening manner. Listen carefully to the students' comments and record them whether you agree with them or not. It is not necessary to implement every change suggested and it may even be unwise to do so. However, it is necessary to consider the recommendations seriously and objectively.

A general checklist for observing is presented in Fig. 7.2. It is possible to generate a matrix for observing the lesson, with the code for each display along one dimension and a list of items to check (for example, overwrites, adequate feedback) along the other. The matrix is an efficient tool for identifying the location and the type of problem, but has the disadvantage of not allowing space to record the nature of the problem, such as an unanticipated correct answer that was judged wrong.

Revisions.   Major revisions are made either after each student trial or after a fixed number of student trials. The decision about when to do the revisions depends on the nature of the problem. If the student reaches a point where the program does not allow her to proceed or keeps repeating the same section over and over, there is no point in having more student trials until after the error has been corrected. If the student is having difficulties understanding the content or is operating at a low level of correct responses, you may want to try the lesson with a few more students before making revisions. The difficulty may lie just with this particular student. If a number of students find the same part difficult, major revisions are warranted. If you have to make major revisions anyhow, you might just as well make minor revisions at the same time. Otherwise, make minor revisions at one time, as noted in the model (Fig. 7.1).

If no major revisions are necessary, it is most efficient to make minor revisions after all of the individual student trials are completed.

Checklist for Trials

1. Observation

A. *Programming.*   Look for execution errors, incorrect answers that are accepted as correct, correct answers that are not accepted, typographical errors, overwrites, incorrect branching, and dead ends.

B. *Communication.*   Is the student able to proceed through the lesson without having to turn to the lesson designer to ask, "What do I do now?" or "What do you mean by this?"

2. Interviews

A. *Colleague:* Ask about adequacy and accuracy of content, and suggestions that might improve the presentation, such as a particularly effective teaching technique.

B. *Student:* Ask about task difficulty, maintenance of interest, sources of confusion, best and worst parts, and suggestions for changes.

3. Caution

A. Initially, test only one student at a time so as to provide your undivided attention.

B. DO NOT try to do the interview while the trial student is doing the lesson. Have the patience to wait until he is finished. Take notes about disturbing points to aid your later interview.

FIG. 7.2   Items to consider during trials of lesson by individuals.

Field trial.   After the major and minor revisions have been completed and you are satisfied that the lesson has been revised to the point where most students reach the criterion you have set, do the field trial. The number of students recommended varies from 5 to 15. Plan to interview the group after this trial in much the same way as you conducted earlier interviews.

The field trial is a good time to determine whether the lesson meets the goal set for the students. If a posttest has been included at the end of the lesson, check the data for consistency between performance during instruction and performance on the posttest. If the students perform well during instruction and not on the posttest, discuss the evaluation measures with the students to determine why this inconsistency exists. It may be that the instruction does not adequately cover some of the material measured by the test. It is also possible that the questions are poorly designed.

SUMMATIVE EVALUATION

Purpose

Summative evaluation takes place after the lesson has been revised and is being used in the intended environment, to help determine how effectively the lesson accomplishes its goals. The data can disclose how well the class as a whole performs, how individual students perform, and, implicitly, how well the lesson works.

Measures

The measures employed are those that were planned and perfected earlier, during the formative evaluation. Recall that the measures obtained by the computer include some or all of the following: time in the lesson, time in individual units, performance on a posttest, performance in units, completion rate, and student attitude toward the lesson.

Reports to Instructors

Since CAI lessons are an integral part of the curriculum, instructors should be informed how well the students are performing. Do not overwhelm the instructor with lots of data even if the computer can and does collect it. Report the data in a form that is useful and usable by the instructor. What is useful depends in part on the goals of the lesson. If the purpose is to provide supplementary instruction and practice on concepts, some instructors may only want to know which students completed the lesson. Other instructors may want summary performance data by topic. An instructor might use data about the nature of students' errors to provide more careful treatment in the classroom in areas of students' weakness.

In some educational settings, such as elementary school, it is useful to provide diagnostic information in addition to the summaries: the names of students who are performing below an acceptable level, and the topics that are causing the difficulty for each of them. The objective is to provide the instructors with all the information needed for diagnosis rather than expect them to infer it from the data. The author of a CAI drill program in arithmetic might prepare teachers' manuals to accompany the CAI lessons. The summative data given the teacher can include the name of each student who requires remediation, the skill in which the student needs the help, and the page in the manual that has examples of the types of problems the student is failing. Such information helps teachers to find example problems for remediation, and they are more likely to follow up the diagnostic reports with corrective instruction.

Reports to Students

Students like to know how well they are doing and how they compare to the rest of the class, particularly with respect to a series of CAI lessons. One experienced professor/lesson designer finds that when he adds to his CAI lessons the option of seeing this information, students' reports of satisfaction with the course increase.

MAINTENANCE

Lessons need to be maintained and data should be collected through on-line reporting and/or classroom monitoring. In some subject areas such as social studies, information may need to be updated. New program errors may occur. Better ways of presenting the material may be identified. Even minor revisions may clarify or improve the lesson. Characteristics of the target population may change. Somebody must be responsible for keeping the lesson in working condition.

DOCUMENTATION

If you expect your lesson to be widely but appropriately used, provide a documentation. In addition to the title, provide your name and institutional affiliation, the year the lesson was written or last revised, the copyright information, the goals, prerequisites, supplementary materials needed, and intended target population. You may have included some, if not all, of this information in the initial displays of your lesson. Off-line documentation, such as a brochure that accompanies the lesson, should include all of the above and a few more items. These include the instructional techniques used, special features, number of students who tested the completed lesson, and results of student trials. An example of a special feature is the use of graphics to illustrate concepts. Documentation is most effective if you state how the special feature enhances learning. Of course, you have to inform the potential user which computer system your lesson requires.

8 Games, Drills, and Simulations

DEFINITIONS

CAI is a medium which is so well suited for presenting highly interactive instruction that it lends itself admirably to games, drills, and simulations. A drill is a lesson that provides practice of materials already learned, in order to strengthen or maintain rote knowledge such as foreign-language vocabulary or arithmetic facts. A game is an educational activity presented in a game format. Success in a game may require only rote knowledge or it may involve the application and extension of knowledge. A simulation is a lesson that approximates or models a real situation in which the student must accomplish a nonroutine task, such as managing the care of a sick patient or finding a faulty part in an electronic circuit. Success in the simulation task requires the application and synthesis of knowledge and the integration of new knowledge with old.

Games, drills, and simulations are not mutually exclusive forms of instruction. Both drills and simulations may be presented in game format. For example, practice counting from 1 to 25 may be just a drill in which the student writes the numbers in order and is judged correct or incorrect after each response. Practice counting may take the form of a dot-to-dot game in which the computer draws lines to connect pairs of successive numbers after the student writes them correctly. If the student counts correctly, the result is a picture, such as a boat or the face of a clown.

The potential motivational and instructional benefits of games, drills, and simulations are manifold. However, neither motivation nor learning takes place automatically merely because the potential exists. Inappropriate

144

games may have no effect on learning or motivation; they may even have negative effects. However, applying instructional design principles increases the probability that games and simulations will, in fact, fulfill expectations. A discussion of these principles follows.

GAMES

Two aspects of games must be considered: their motivational appeal to the students and their educational effectiveness. These are obviously not mutually exclusive components. A game may be fun but not necessarily instructive. On the other hand, a game may be instructive but boring. How can an author create games that are both motivating and educationally effective?

Educational Aspects of Games

Extrinsically instructional. In some games the subject matter and the game context are entirely independent. The game is instructional, since students receive practice and may improve in performance as a consequence. The game context itself does not contribute to the learning. The purpose of the game is motivation, and the game itself is extrinsic to the actual learning. This type of game is extrinsically instructional.

Success in such extrinsically instructional games depends on the student's ability to recall facts or rote information. Performance is evaluated by the computer. The feedback is judgmental rather than corrective: the answer is right or wrong.

One example is a very popular arithmetic drill in game format called Speedway, developed for the PLATO CAI system by Seiler. The context is an automobile race (Fig. 8.1). The student is the driver of a car that races against another car with the goal of being the first to cross the finish line. The other car is "driven" by the computer, using the data from the student's previous record. Arithmetic problems are presented one at a time, and the student answers as quickly as possible. The faster the answer, the further the car travels, provided the answer is correct. If the student's answer is incorrect, not only does his car not move, but the student loses time entering the correct answer.

The student must recall rote knowledge in order to succeed in this game; he does not have to know how to race a car in order to win; he only has to know the arithmetic fact. The computer tells him if the answer is right or wrong. Moreover, the fact that the car did not move because the answer was wrong does not help the student learn the correct answer. Although the lesson provides remedial assistance when the student needs it, this remediation is entirely outside the context of the speedway. The function of

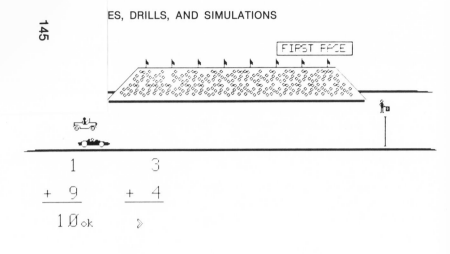

FIG. 8.1 Display from an extrinsically instructional game. (From computer-assisted instruction lesson, *Speedway*. Copyright © 1976 by The Board of Trustees of the University of Illinois. Reprinted by permission.)

this type of game format is to motivate the student and to improve speed in using existing knowledge.

Intrinsically instructional. Intrinsically instructional games differ from extrinsically instructional in that the game context itself provides instruction as well as motivation. Performance on the task is an intrinsic part of the game. The student can see for herself how well she is doing without having to depend on the computer to tell her if the answer is right or wrong. To win the game, the student must make new applications of available knowledge or gain new knowledge, such as generating a problem-solving strategy.

An example of an intrinsically instructional game is another by Seiler on the PLATO system, entitled "How the West Was Won." Two players take turns moving their pieces across a board by constructing an arithmetic expression from three numbers randomly generated by spinners. The distance moved is equal to the value of the expression (Fig. 8.2). The goal is to be the first one to reach a town at the end of the trail on the board. Certain moves, such as landing on a town along the trail, have advantages.

In order to win, students must do more than recall facts; they must synthesize many aspects of their knowledge. The results are self-evident from the context of the game. The distance the student moves is neither right nor wrong; it depends on the expression she generates. If the spinners show the numbers 2, 3, and 4, for example, the student will move only 14 spaces if she enters the expression $3 \times 4 + 2$. However, she can move 18 spaces by entering the response 3 × (4 + 2) and move 20 spaces if she chooses 4 × (3 + 2). The student's chances of winning depend on the context of the game as well as on her arithmetic skills.

Such an intrinsically instructional game seems to be a unique opportunity for new learning, in which students can acquire new strategies by modeling their opponent or by making inferences from the results of their own strategies. However, the limited research available shows that this new learning does not actually occur.

Do people learn from games?   Results of research based on actual data are presented first and are followed by a report of the observations made by experienced CAI authors/instructors.

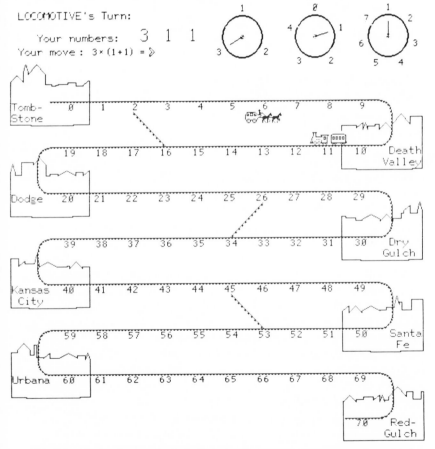

FIG. 8.2   Display from an intrinsically instructional game. (From computer-assisted instruction lesson, *How the West Was Won*. Copyright © 1976 by The Board of Trustees of the University of Illinois. Reprinted by permission.)

Non-CAI educational games have been used in schools with the obvious expectation that they would facilitate learning and have positive affective outcomes, as well. However, one study in the use of games and other adjunct materials (for example, puzzles) in second and third grades in California schools showed a negative relationship between their use and student performance. Three reasons were suggested for this situation: (1) The games lacked motivational value for the learners. (2) The games did not provide activity that was pertinent to the learning. Some teachers, for example, used the games as a reward after the instruction and learning in the content matter had already been completed. (3) The games were not necessarily pertinent to the skills the students were learning; either the game was not appropriate for the goal, or the teacher taught a method different from the one the students had to use in the game.

A study of eight "educational microprocessor games" used in four schools in New York City also showed negative results. Standardized tests demonstrated no significant pretest-posttest gains in either spelling or arithmetic. It was reported that the content of the games did not correlate well with the curriculum below the fifth grade. None of the children below that grade could do the multiplication or division required in the games. The younger children could not even cope with addition and subtraction in horizontal ($3 + 4 =$ ____) rather than vertical ($\begin{smallmatrix} 3 \\ +\,4 \end{smallmatrix}$) form. In spelling, none of the children learned words they had not known before, even after two or three tries. All of the children became bored, even those who heard a "pleasant beep" when they spelled a word correctly.

In a military setting students studied two different topics via CAI, powers of ten and formula solving. No significant differences in performance or training time were found between using conventional lessons and the two different game formats of the lessons.

The games employed in both the elementary school and the military studies were extrinsically instructional. Now, let us consider games that are intrinsically instructional.

One study showed that elementary-school students who played the game "How the West Was Won" did not generate new strategies for winning the game. Students tended to develop a limited strategy and use it repeatedly, whether or not it helped them win the game. From the perspective of learning new strategies for manipulating number combinations, the game was not instructionally effective. No data are available on performance in computational skills, since measuring them was not the purpose of the research.

Informal observations of students playing CAI estimation games have shown that although students find the games highly motivating, they do not learn new or better estimation skills even after extensive experience. The students failed to make use of cues that were provided in the game. Conversations with the students indicated that they were capable of using these cues but did not use them until the observer showed them how to do so. Furthermore, it was not clear that they would use these cues at another time, particularly if not required to. It seems that the goals of the game were not necessarily the same, for elementary-school children, at least, as for the author. The author wanted the students to learn to be very efficient in winning the game; the students just wanted to win and didn't care about being efficient, even though they lost the game some of the times.

A computer lesson can be written to give students advice on good strategies for winning a game, but there is no guarantee that students will follow it. One program was designed to give students hints on how to play the game "How the West Was Won." The advice was based on the computer's model of differences between the strategies employed by the student and those that would be employed by an expert player. Twelve student teachers tested this advice-giving lesson. Nine of them thought that the advice given by the computer was appropriate, but no data were reported on how well the twelve performed. Thus, we really do not know if even these adult students followed the advice presented by the computer.

One shortcoming of this advice-giving program is that the expert used only one strategy for moving: get the furthest distance ahead of the opponent. A student may have been using a different strategy and been unwilling to give it up in favor of the one being promoted by the computer advisor. Alternatively, a student may have been using several different strategies, depending on the particular conditions of the moment.

CAI authors have often designed games to provide practice for their students in college courses. In their reports these authors have described the games and reported that students liked them. Usually no other data have accompanied the reports, and for good reason. The lesson designers did not expect superior performance as a result of practice obtained playing games over practice obtained in other ways. They simply wanted to make the practice as appealing as possible, to help their students achieve competence in the subject matter. For the most part, the games were extrinsically instructional. The function of these games was to motivate the students to practice, and thereby to improve performance.

An exception is found in some of the chemistry games authored by Stanley Smith and Ruth Chabay. Their goal was to provide practice, but many of their games were also intrinsically instructional, often involving interterminal competition. In one game students challenged each other by giving the name of an element or its chemical symbol. The opponent had to respond with either the symbol or the name. If the response was correct, the opponent got points equal to the atomic number of the element, and the first player to reach 1000 points won. This game is intrinsically instructional because students must draw on and integrate additional information (atomic number) about the elements in order to keep the opponent's score low. The authors reported that many students liked these games because they provided needed practice and enabled the students to learn from others in a competitive, but personally anonymous, format.

Structured games were the teaching tecnique chosen by Moshell and his colleagues to teach basic concepts in computer science to average students. The authors stated the following criteria for the design of their games:

1. The author must specify a set of concepts and skills that the student is supposed to learn as a consequence of playing the game. The author makes a plan for how the game teaches these skills.

2. The content that the student learns in each activity becomes part of a cumulative body of knowledge.

3. Each game is superseded by another which is more interesting and more interactive, and which the student cannot handle unless he has mastered the skills taught in the previous game.

According to the definitions presented here, these games are intrinsically instructional. Particularly appealing is the principle that the author must have a plan for how each game teaches. The author does not assume that somehow the student will learn but, instead, arranges the game to help the student learn.

Motivational Aspects of Games

This section derives almost exclusively from the research of Thomas Malone. He distinguished between intrinsic and extrinsic motivation. An activity is intrinsically motivating if there is no obvious external reward; it is extrinsically motivating if there is some form of reward, such as money or social reinforcement. In an extensive study of children's preferences among CAI games, Malone found three characteristics of intrinsically motivating games: challenge, fantasy, and curiosity.

To be challenging, a game must have a goal that is obvious to the player, a goal that includes multiple-goal levels. An uncertain outcome is an important aspect of challenge, as when there is an element of chance (for example, the numbers on the spinners in "How the West Was Won"). Hidden information can also add challenge to a game. Games are the most challenging when there is no known optimal strategy. In some games, such as NIM, however, specific strategies always work; only the first player can win if both players employ these strategies. Such a limitation diminishes the challenge and hence the motivational quality of the game.

Fantasy is a situation that evokes mental images. In extrinsic fantasy the student does not need skill in the fantasy to succeed in the task, but skill in the task. In intrinsic fantasy, exercise of the skill depends on the fantasy, too. The Speedway game is an example of an extrinsic fantasy; the game "How the West Was Won" is an example of an intrinsic fantasy. Both kinds of fantasies are motivating.

An element that piques curiosity also makes a game motivating. Curiosity involves an element of novelty, though not so "far out" that the novelty is totally incomprehensible. Curiosity also involves reducing uncertainty about the state of the world. For example, it is curiosity that leads a person to finish reading a mystery story, unable to set it aside after reading all except the last chapter.

Implications for Designing CAI Games

Why bother with games? There are no data to show that students learn better from games than from other instructional formats. Students at the college level, in general, learn whatever rote knowledge they have to, boring or not. In addition, games take extra time to program.

Nevertheless, even good learners among college students enjoy motivating games in learning. Why not make learning rote materials as pleasant as possible? Furthermore, it may be that games really do help some students significantly. Those who are low performers in the subject area (for example, foreign language) may need the extra motivation to carry them through the course. There are no research data to support this premise, but neither do data exist to reject it.

At the elementary-school level, games have frequently been ineffective educationally, although they were often motivating. The major reasons for this failure have been (1) poor design of the games, (2) use at inappropriate grade levels, and (3) lack of coordination with classroom instruction. It is possible that games can be an effective instructional device if properly developed and properly implemented. It is also possible that students learn other things from games than those objectives we anticipate or measure. Games should not be summarily discarded just because all of the educational outcomes cannot be measured. Rather, authors should design games according to the best available knowledge, aware that their educational effectiveness may be difficult to predict.

Production of intrinsically instructional games are discussed here. Extrinsically instructional games are basically drills and are discussed under "Drills."

What to do. The following are steps for developing intrinsically instructional games:

1. Specify the concepts and skills the student should acquire as a consequence of playing the game.

The author does not begin by designing a "great" game and then assume that the student will learn the subject matter just because the format is a game. The first step is to decide what the student should learn. As in the design of any instruction, the author must have a clear idea of the purpose of the game.

2. Specify where the game fits into the overall sequence of instruction.

When generating a game, the author makes certain assumptions about the knowledge and skills the student must have in order to play. State precisely the first point in the curriculum at which the student should have this background and consequently be ready for the game.

3. Design activities which will help the student learn the designated skills and concepts.

Do not leave learning to chance. Design activities that help the student learn the material, and specify how each activity can aid in learning. This designing does not mean "tell them and ask them." Rather, it means that the activities must be such that the student has to apply or integrate the new information with other knowledge in order to do the task. It may mean that the author must also provide hints and corrective feedback to help the student who needs it.

4. Reformulate the activities in the format of a motivational game. Once the instruction has been designed, make it motivating by incorporating features that make games motivating, as noted.

How to do it.   State precisely and exactly the goals the student should reach, and make those goals clear and obvious to the student. You may wish to specify goals with increasing levels of difficulty to make the game more challenging for individual students as they improve their skills.

Decide on the prerequisites for the game. What skills and knowledge are really essential in order to benefit from it? Every game cannot be educationally effective for every knowledge (or grade) level. As noted previously, one of the serious flaws in currently available commercial CAI games is that they are not realistic about the knowledge needed to play the games. Some children do not learn from them because they simply do not have an adequate background.

The activity you design should require students to apply old knowledge in a new way or to synthesize various parts of their knowledge. If possible, the activity should be such that students can judge for themselves how well they are performing. Generate constructive hints or corrective feedback sequences to help students who need them.

Make the activity into a motivating game by adding an element of fantasy. Insert an element of uncertainty so that the players do not know for sure if they will win or lose. Arouse the students' curiosity by including a hidden element. Clearly, the author of a CAI game will not be able to apply every suggestion to every game, due to differences in subject matter, goals, computer power, and target populations. Do try to include some of them.

An Example

1. Specify the goal. The sample game has three goals: (a) For any specified area under 100 square units, state a pair of numbers whose product is equivalent to that area. (b) For any number less than or equal to 100, judge whether it has more than one pair of factors. (c) State alternate pairs of numbers, when possible, whose product is equivalent to a given area.

2. Specify where these goals fit into the curriculum. The student must have already completed a lesson demonstrating the relationship between areas and multiplication tables, using a bulletin board covered with square sheets of paper as the model (Fig. 8.3).

3. Design an activity in which the student applies the desired knowledge. Be cognizant of how the activity will help the student reach the goal. One activity is to have the computer generate an area and ask the student to type two numbers whose product will give that area (Fig. 8.4). A second activity is to ask the student to type as many pairs of numbers as he can for a given area.

```
                              DIRECTIONS

            Make a bulletin-board that has an area of
            12 squares.
```

Bulletin Board			
1	2	3	4

```
            Here is the top row of the bulletin-board.

            Tell PLATO how many rows to draw. >
```

FIG. 8.3 Preliminary activity for multiplication game. (From computer-assisted instruction lesson, *Rectangles, Areas, and Multiplication.* Copyright © 1976 by The Board of Trustees of the University of Illinois. Reprinted by permission.)

```
            Press -LAB- if you want to change
            the number of squares in a row.
            Press -HELP- if you need it.
```

A 4×6 rectangle has 24 squares.
A 7×8 rectangle has 56 squares.
A ▷   rectangle has 10 squares.

1	2	3	4	5	6	7	8	9	10	11	12
2	4	6	8	10	12	14	16	18	20	22	24
3	6	9	12	15	18	21	24	27	30	33	36
4	8	12	16	20	24	28	32	36	40	44	48
5	10	15	20	25	30	35	40	45	50	55	60
6	12	18	24	30	36	42	48	54	60	66	72
7	14	21	28	35	42	49	56	63	70	77	84
8	16	24	32	40	48	56	64	72	80	88	96
9	18	27	36	45	54	63	72	81	90	99	108
10	20	30	40	50	60	70	80	90	100	110	120
11	22	33	44	55	66	77	88	99	110	121	132
12	24	36	48	60	72	84	96	108	120	132	144

FIG. 8.4   Preliminary activity for multiplication game. (From computer-assisted instruction lesson, *Rectangles, Areas, and Multiplication.* Copyright © 1976 by The Board of Trustees of the University of Illinois. Reprinted by permission.)

4. Add a game format. Challenge can be added in the following ways:

(a) Make the game a competition between two students. The first one to reach 500 points wins.

(b) Generate multiple goals. In addition to finding the factors, find the one with the greatest sum. If the student gives a correct answer, give him the number of points that is equal to the sum of the two factors. (If the number is not prime, do not allow the number itself and 1.) For example, if the area is 20, either 4 × 5 or 10 × 2 is correct. (The rules excluded 20 × 1.) However, the sum of 4 and 5 is 9, whereas the sum of 10 and 2 is 12. The student who responds 10 × 2 will get more points that the one who responds 4 × 5. Thus, we have added motivation for considering all possible pairs of factors.

(c) Make the outcome uncertain: let the computer generate the areas randomly.

(d) Add other levels of difficulty. For example, in one version allow students to use factors that are not shown on the bulletin board. The area, 42 square units, has the factors 6 and 7 (shown on the table) and also 21 and 2 (not shown on the table). The game can also be made more difficult by removing the digits in the top row and in the left-hand column. This format forces the student to recall the factors without seeing them. Some students will simply count the number of rows and columns if the top and left-hand ones are removed and they can't recall the factors. The lesson author can circumvent this shortcut by putting a limit on the time allowed for the response.

Notice that the random element in the game precludes the expectation that students will get practice finding factors of every number. It is not possible to predict the amount of practice or the level of expertise the student will gain toward the first goal. However, we are more confident that students will meet the second and third goals, since they are an integral part of winning the game. For students who have difficulty winning, the author may include an optional section to use, between games, that teaches the student the strategy for the game.

DRILLS

As noted previously, drills are exercises that help students maintain or strengthen knowledge they already have, such as the symbols of the chemical elements or the names of the bones in the human leg. CAI is an ideal medium for presenting drills, since it can respond to individualized needs in many ways: informing the student whether each answer is right or wrong, keeping a record of missed items for later presentation, presenting additional practice as needed, and adjusting the speed of presentation when that element is an important goal. The computer can also be programmed to present the information-to-be-learned in a manner that will make it easier to remember, or it can teach certain memory strategies such as mnemonic devices.

In this text drills refer to rote memory tasks, particularly those in which a stimulus is shown and the student gives a fixed response, such as English word (stimulus) — French equivalent (response).

Decisions the Author Must Make

Order of presentation of items.   The author must decide how to manage the pool of items: whether to present them randomly or not; if randomly presented, whether to put those done incorrectly back in the item pool or keep a record and present the missed items at the end of the set.

Help.   The author must also decide whether to provide remedial help in the drill, perhaps by teaching some memory strategies to the student or arranging the conditions of the drill to facilitate memory.

Control.   The author must decide who will control the drill, the student or the computer. If the computer controls the drill, the author makes decisions about criteria for successful completion. Many of these decisions will be dictated by the author's purpose in generating the drill. If the purpose of the lesson is to provide students a self-learning aid to use as they choose, allow the students considerable control over the drill. This method has been used for many college-level foreign-language lessons, as noted previously. If the material to be learned is difficult, the lesson designer may specify a required level of performance and generate an algorithm for presenting items in the drill.

Management.   It is not always possible to specify the most helpful drill a priori, and the designer may want to compare some alternatives before making such a decision.

The authors of one CAI drill compared two alternative methods of management, both designed to help students recall the symbols associated with sounds of the International Phonetic Alphabet. In both versions of the lesson, sounds were randomly selected. In one of the drills, if a student typed the wrong response, she was not allowed to continue until she entered the correct one. The student worked until she did 12 of the preceding 14 succesive items correctly. In the other version of the drill, each item missed was returned to the item pool for later presentation. The criterion for success in this drill was fewer than two items wrong on the first try. Results showed that although both groups learned the material adequately, those who repeated missed items performed significantly better on a subsequent off-line transcription test. Thus, for this subject matter and for these students, both drills enabled students to achieve the minimum goal, but one drill produced significantly better results than the minimum performance.

Implications for Generating Drills

It should be clear from this discussion that there is no "best" way to present a drill. Several alternatives may be equally satisfactory. The suggestions that follow derived from authors' reports of their experiences with CAI drills.

First, an admonition about long-term usefulness of a drill: It is not practical to generate drills that are tied to the specific content and sequence of one textbook. When that textbook is replaced by another, some parts of the drill will be inapplicable. Therefore, generate content (for example, vocabulary) that is usually presented in most textbooks.

Number of items.   Keep the number of items relatively short, particularly if criterion for success is high (for example, 90% correct on the first try) or if the students are poor or immature learners. If drills are relatively short, students will be able to complete them within reasonable time frames. In addition, if drills are short it will be easier to assign students to the particular content they need to practice.

Variety.   If the students are likely to require repeated practice on certain sets of items, design a variety of formats. Do not, however, switch formats within a drill. For example, a set of 10 items may first be presented as a matching exercise and then be followed by a multiple-choice drill on the same 10 items.

Index.   Provide an index for accessing the drills. In this way an instructor can assign a student to appropriate drills and not require him to repeat sections he already knows.

Avoid heavy-handedness.   Students will not want to be forced to do an annoyingly repetitive drill for any length of time even if it is presented on a computer. Set the criterion for performance realistically. Suppose, in a given drill, that items are returned to the item pool. Suppose, further, that an item is permanently removed from the pool only after it has been presented and answered correctly on three successive presentations. The student answers correctly on the first two such repeats but makes a typographical error on the third attempt. Following the stated rule, the computer must present the item again at least three more times. Such repetition is not only aggravating but a waste of the student's time. Many students, in fact, will not complete such a drill.

If the author chooses to allow the student control over the drill, an index of topics is essential. A keypress must be designated for exiting any drill and returning to the index. Be sure to tell the student which key to use. Display the name of the key and its function on every display, if possible. On the index display, mark each topic that the student has completed.

Motivation.   A simple motivator is a display of the student's progress, such as the number of items completed and the number of items remaining to be done. If the material to be learned is difficult or the students are poor learners, motivate by giving some credit for a correct answer on a second attempt, though less than for an initial success. For instance, set a goal of a certain number of points and give 5 points for getting the answer right on the first try and 2 points on the second try. Another motivator for some populations is competition with other students or with a student's own previous performance. Add fantasy — for example, the accumulation of points can be shown as a flame burning up a wick to a fireworks display. When the goal is reached, the fireworks go off.

SIMULATIONS

Definition

A simulation is a model of an event: a process or an abstract idea. The event may be physically observable or not; it may have occurred in the past or reflect an estimate of future occurrence; it may represent reality in every detail or only in a subset of features.

Educational Purposes

The instructional purposes of using simulations generally fall into two broad categories: (1) to teach principles or complex concepts, or (2) to teach processes and skills. CAI simulations occur in both categories.

Insights about complex scientific principles often come from experience with such concepts in an interactive environment. However, students may be unable to interact directly with certain physical phenomena, such as the waning and waxing of the moon. A pheomenon may require a long time to transpire in real life, but time can be compressed in a simulation, enabling the student to make observations of the outcomes. A person cannot experience an event that took place in the past, such as travel on the Oregon trail. Nor is it possible to experience the future, such as the social consequences of present demographic trends and the availability of world food supplies. Simulations afford a powerful tool for teaching historical, complex, and often abstract matters.

Teaching a process or skill may be costly if it takes place in the real environment. It may be more inexpensively accomplished through simulation, as in some aspects of training airplane pilots. Applying a skill without previous experience may have dangerous consequences, as in the management and care of a sick person. A simulation can bridge the gap between book or classroom knowledge and practical experience in the real world.

Experience Using CAI Simulations for Instruction

Common threads run through the experiences of those who have generated CAI simulations, across different computer systems and in various content domains.

First and foremost is that a simulation must include enough guidance or advice to help the student attain the stated goals.

Most of the authors who developed CAI simulations to teach procedural skills had previous experience teaching the particular content, and were actively seeking a way of teaching some specific processes that students were not learning under current modes of instruction. Instructors in teacher-training programs wanted to give student teachers practical experience diagnosing and remedying children's reading problems or managing teaching strategies in mathematics, before working with real children. In these simulations the students were given choices to make from a finite set of alternatives. The computer program provided various degrees of hints, feedback, and corrective information to help them learn from this experience.

By contrast, most lesson designers who developed simulations to teach principles did not initially generate specific goals for the students. They provided the simulation and allowed students the freedom to "explore alternatives" or "experience the consequences of their actions." However, students were not likely to learn the basic ideas and concepts when the author failed to provide some kind of guidance. In a simulation of a union leader's negotiating a contract with a school board, students had to repeat the lesson several times in order to infer the main ideas; some students never did learn them. In physics lessons concerning motion, students entered parameters randomly rather than systematically and derived little benefit from the simulation. Sometimes, simulations of principles were not generated for a specific target population but were intended to be used by anybody who happened to be studying that subject. As a consequence, student performance was not as high as had been anticipated. Integration and customization of specific simulation lessons for specific courses was recommended, rather than a library of general simulations.

Another experience reported by designers of simulations was a difficulty attributable to lack of adequate computing capacity. The computer not only had to store vast amounts of data but also had to do a considerable amount of computation to analyze students' responses, in order to give appropriate feedback. In some instances there were long delays in computer response time. In other instances (on a large centrally controlled CAI system) there was such a heavy load on the system that only a few students could work simultaneously. In a simulation of flying in a holding pattern, the computer system was unable to analyze all the data fast enough to give adequate corrective feedback to the students during the lesson. Other problems arose because the interaction between the student and the simulation was cumbersome.

In simulations developed on the PLATO system, excessive emphasis on realistic details diverted the students' attention from the important to the insignificant aspects of the subject.

Implications for Designing Simulations

1. The lesson designer must have a specific goal for the students. Begin with a limited goal; don't try to accomplish too much at first. CAI simulations require an enormous amount of development time and effort.

2. Think of the simulation as an integral part of a particular course of study, for a particular target population. Define the preliminary or background material that precedes the simulation and the expected instructional medium, such as another CAI lesson, specific readings, or laboratory experiments. Specify the mode of the follow-up discussions, such as on-line or classroom.

3. Provide the students with sufficient guidance or advice to direct their studies. This guidance has two aspects: (a) instructions about the technical aspects, the mechanics of executing the simulation, and (b) guidance about how to learn from it.

3a. Provide clear and precise directions about how to interact with the simulation. Enable the students to interact easily with any external devices. General techniques for helping the student interact with the lesson have been discussed earlier. Techniques for dealing with specialized external devices, such as music generators or joy stick, are beyond the scope of this text.

Students are likely to do a simulation lesson more than one time. Allow the option of bypassing the instructions and going directly to the simulation if they have done the lesson previously. This option can be readily accomplished by inserting a display such as the following:

Do you want to see the directions?
Type *y* or *n*.

3b. It is the responsibility of the lesson designer to orient, guide, and evaluate students in the cognitive aspects of a CAI simulation. The lesson should help students learn how to decide what information to seek, what questions to ask in order to obtain that information, and how to make inferences about what to do next from the feedback given to their questions. If students have little or no knowledge about the principles to be learned, how can they be expected to know what information is relevant? If they must seek information by trial and error, how can they be expected to make inferences about the implications of the feedback?

The guidance you, the author, provide is partly dependent on the purpose of the simulation. If students are to gain a better understanding of the variation of some physical phenomenon, make suggestions about ways to get started. For example, they might enter certain values (perhaps boundary conditions) and describe the resulting effects on the phenomenon under discussion. Continue to give hints about other sets of values they could enter. When they have gathered sufficient data, ask them to make inferences about the principle you are trying to simulate. Be specific in the questions. Allow students to gather more data if they wish to do so. If the simulation is teaching a skill, present a list of procedures or activities they can choose and suggest an efficient order or sequence in which to do them. Provide feedback on students' performance and suggest ways of improving it. Feedback may be immediate, as part of the simulation, or it may be delayed and presented as a debriefing after the simulation is completed.

Guidance may be provided on-line, or off-line by printed materials, classroom discussions, or any combination thereof. Any of the suggestions presented above may be implemented on-line: suggestions about what to do, questions about findings, hints, corrective feedback, and debriefing. Printed materials may include information about features of the lesson or give an overview or "map" of the simulation if it is rather complex. Printed materials may suggest supplementary or related activities, such as library projects or role playing. Though useful and important, such activities do not help the student meet the instructional goals of the CAI lesson. Printed materials should ask questions about the lesson itself.

Pertinent printed materials may include such items as a format for recording observations, decisions, or data. Include questions asking the student to interpret the data. If you are simulating the hazards of travel in covered wagons, ask students which of their decisions would most likely account for their reaching, or failing to reach, their destination. Ask how they would do things differently if they were to undertake the trip again, and how this reasoning is supported by their experience. Suggest that they do the lesson again to evaluate the quality of their decisions, or tell them to compare their decisions and the consequences with those of other students.

Guidance in a simulation may also be provided by a classroom demonstration and discussion, presented before students do the simulation individually. This discussion would obviously include the kind of directions suggested earlier for deriving the maximum benefit.

Evaluation of Learning from Simulations

It is sometimes difficult to evaluate simulation lessons. Some simulations, particularly those that teach principles, have no real ending—they allow students to enter information and observe reactions as many times as desired. Testing students on the application and synthesis of knowledge learned may have to be done at a later time, off-line. Consequently, it may be difficult to attribute a successful performance to the simulation alone, rather than to the simulation in conjunction with other learning resources. An informal but useful source of evaluation is a questionnaire asking students for their perceptions of the usefulness of the simulation.

Simulations that teach a skill are easier to evaluate. One method is to generate two forms of the simulation, one that gives the student continuous feedback (for learning) and one that gives no feedback (for testing). Another alternative is to give pretests and posttests. Finally, subsequent performance in the real situation can be evaluated.

CARDINAL PRINCIPLE: Games, drills, and simulations are not automatically motivating or educationally effective for the average student. Special instructional conditions must be designed to increase the probability that the students will learn from such lessons.

9

Efficiency, Implementation, and Learning How to Learn

EFFICIENCY

It should be clear by now that CAI lesson authoring is a long and time-consuming process, particularly for the beginner. Obviously, CAI designers are exploring ways of expediting the process while maintaining high standards. The two major time-consuming elements of lesson development are the instructional design process itself and the computer programming. Systems for developing a general instructional design process have been generated for both CAI and non-CAI. Systems are also being developed to bypass the need for an expert programmer and thus minimize the amount of technical or programming expertise the author needs in order to program the lesson. Advantages and disadvantages of these systems are discussed below. In addition to these systems, there are some techniques that experienced programmers have developed to speed up the development of CAI lessons, which are also presented.

Authoring Languages

An authoring language is a programming language that includes specific commands useful for CAI. Many computer languages, such as BASIC, do not have any commands that judge a student's answer. To write a CAI lesson using BASIC, every time you want to judge the student's answer you must write some code to tell the computer how to decide if the student's response is correct. The author has to teach the computer how to judge responses. In contrast, an authoring language like PILOT or TUTOR has commands for judging purposes, so that the author does not have to teach the computer how to check to see if the answer is correct. An authoring language makes it easier to program a CAI lesson, but an author still has to learn that language and do the programming.

Author-Prompting Systems

An author-prompting system is an interactive system enabling an author with a minimum knowledge of programming languages to create a CAI lesson. The system prompts the author: It asks the author what message to display, what answers to accept as correct, what feedback to display contingent on particular responses and so on. The system then generates the lesson according to these specifications.

The advantage of an author-prompting system is obvious: You can generate a complete lesson by yourself without having to acquire programming expertise. You can make program changes yourself whenever they are needed, without explaining them to a programmer and waiting for him to implement them. Thus, using such a system can save a considerable amount of time and trouble, and ensure that needed revisions will actually be made. It is difficult to evaluate the extent to which author-prompting systems will actually fulfill their promise. System flexibility, system computing capacity, and the quality of the instructional designs they can accommodate—all will affect their potential. Author-prompting systems cannot provide the flexibility that is available to a programmer. For example, they cannot accommodate every kind of lesson an author may wish to generate, such as both tutorials and simulations. Author-prompting systems are most easily used for direct, tutorial instruction: show-and-tell, then ask questions and remediate where necessary. Since a considerable proportion of instruction is presented in this manner, these systems should be time-savers for a large segment of CAI lesson development.

To be acceptable, then, the flexibility required of an author-prompting system is not its ability to handle a wide range of pedagogical formats but rather its flexibility within selected formats. The system must allow authors to implement the design features they would generate if they were doing the programming themselves. Since individualizing instruction is essential, the author should expect to be able to do the following in the system: specify answer-contingent branching, accept all reasonable correct responses, give response-contingent feedback, and keep data as a basis for directing the sequence of instruction. In other words, an author-prompting system must not force the lesson designer to sacrifice the quality of the instructional design because of the lack of authoring options.

A flexible author-prompting system requires a considerable amount of storage capacity. The computer must not only store the student's lesson but also the program that prompts the author and generates the lesson for presentation to the students. The implication is that small microcomputer systems may be unable to transfer large sections of the student's lesson at one time from the disk to the computer system. Consequently, the student may encounter time delays because the computer must frequently transfer information from the disk to the main system. We do not know if these delays will be so long that they disrupt the flow of instruction.

Finally, and perhaps most important: an author-prompting system with considerable flexibility and adequate speed is only part of the requirement for the development of good lessons. Attention and time must always be given to quality instructional design. It is important never to let the speed of implementation with an authoring system mislead you into speeding up the design of the instruction by shortcutting important steps in the procedure.

Systems for Instructional Design

Institutions that must continually produce new instruction for new equipment or new procedures, such as industry or the military, have attempted to make the design process more efficient by eliminating the need for designing instruction for each lesson individually. They generate instructional design systems (IDS) which define the steps that should be taken. Then, to generate instruction, individuals just follow this system rather than take the time to generate their own designs.

This method sounds like a good way to speed up the instructional design process, but it is not without complications and obstacles. An IDS is based on a number of assumptions, some of which are only partially valid. The assumptions will be listed first, and then followed by a discussion of each one individually.

1. We know enough about the learning process to design an IDS.
2. The people who apply the system will understand it well enough to do so reliably.
3. The extensive amount of time that must be invested in generating an IDS will result in a real time savings over individually designed lessons.

Developers of an IDS assume a priori that their design will be effective. An entire instructional curriculum is then developed on this premise. We know something about how to make instruction effective under certain conditions, for certain populations, and for certain subject matter. However, we do not know enough about the learning process to always be able to produce an IDS that will ultimately result in effective lessons. If the design assumptions are invalid, the entire curriculum will be deficient. It is true that once the flaws are identified, revisions can be made. In the meantime, however, all of the numerous lessons generated under this system bear these major deficiencies.

A somewhat different conception of IDS is a general system for designing lessons, one that lists the steps in the procedure but does not define a particular instructional strategy. An IDS typically lists four or five stages, such as definition of objectives, task analysis, lesson design, trial, and revision. The components of each stage are then specified in greater detail. One of the problems that arises in this case is that the IDS tells what to do, but not how to do it. The individuals who implement the system often do not understand it well enough to carry it out reliably. Someone who does not understand why a particular step is in the procedure may simply omit it, and inadvertently change a critical instructional feature of the lesson.

An intensive amount of time must be devoted to generating an IDS. Depending on the extent of success of the initial implementation, additional time is consumed revising and improving it. Consequently, the system must be used for a large number of lessons in order to be cost- and time-effective.

One final comment. There are tradeoffs between using an IDS and designing lessons individually. With an IDS all lessons must be created according to a fixed set of rules, even those that could be better presented in a different way. The general procedure is insensitive to individual situations; though it may not be the best for every situation, it should be satisfactory in many different ones. If you choose to generate an IDS, you gain a savings in the time and cost of producing lessons, but you lose sensitivity to the needs of some of the learning situations. If you choose to design lessons individually, you can be creative and tailor the lessons to suit the specific needs of the content and complexity, but you may need an inordinate amount of time to produce the lessons.

Author-Designed Techniques

Those who choose to design individual lessons can also engage in some efficient, time-saving techniques.

New authors on the PLATO system who were learning to program relied on instructional techniques they had used previously. The lesson learned from their experience is relevant to authors using other computer systems, too: You will become proficient most quickly if you concentrate on one thing at a time. First, concentrate on learning to program and on understanding the features of the CAI system. Try to design instruction that has previously proved effective for you. Hold off on attempting innovative instructional techniques until after you have familiarized yourself with the system.

If you want to use a new teaching technique, invest some time experimenting with different ways of presenting and programming the lesson. Such experimentation should help you become proficient in applying the technique to other lessons. The time thus invested will have long-term benefits.

Some lesson formats, such as games, can be used for more than one content area. The Concentration game, for example, can be used for practice in remembering locations of identical objects, such as pictures of various animals. The game can also be used for identifying equivalent items, such as number combinations that have equivalent values (for example, 6 + 1 and 3 + 4). After you have written the lesson for specific content and evaluated and revised it, you may wish to write a general program, which allows insertion of any subject matter.

IMPLEMENTATION

It is the responsibility of the lesson author to help the teacher implement the lesson in the classroom. This responsibility has somewhat different implications in different educational institutions.

Elementary and Secondary Schools

Acceptance of innovations in public education is relatively slow. Although microcomputer systems are rapidly appearing in schools, many teachers still treat them with suspicion and distrust, especially if the content of the CAI lessons is innovative and different from conventional instruction in some way. Teachers fear they will be replaced by CAI; they are afraid of being embarrassed because they might not know what to do or how to cope with the computer. If, in addition, the CAI lesson is not traditional, they may be afraid they will not be totally in charge of what the children are learning. The moral of the story is: Help promote acceptance and use of your CAI lessons by minimizing the perceived threat to the teacher.

One way to do this is to tell the teacher what's in the lesson, how and where it fits into the curriculum, and how it can most easily be used. Present this information in a way that is directly translatable into practice. For example, state that the lesson is intended to review and practice a concept *after* the teacher has introduced it in class and the students have completed the exercises in the textbook. Transmit this information either on-line or in an instructor's manual.

A teacher's day is totally filled; he has many responsibilities and little time to add new ones. If a lesson is too much trouble, it simply will not be used. Let the teacher know that the students can do the lesson without the teacher's supervision. If the lesson can save the teacher time by tutoring students who have special needs, like remediation or enrichment, be sure to point this out.

Post-Secondary

Post-secondary institutions that provide instruction and training include community colleges, 4-year colleges and universities, industry, and the military. The problem of acceptance should not be as great here as in public schools since CAI is often introduced to fulfill a perceived need. However, there is probably greater diversity in curricula. Thus here, too, it is essential to state explicitly how you expect the lesson to be integrated into the curriculum.

Your lesson should provide the instructor with an index, even if for some reason you have not provided one for the students. Tell the instructor how to access the index and suggest ways he can look through the lesson to get the flavor of it. Note sections that have special features, such as Section 3 is an animation of the flow of fluid when the valves are opened and closed.

LEARNING AND LEARNING HOW TO LEARN

Learning Environments

In the past, the emphasis in school has been on the acquisition of knowledge rather than on the processes required to obtain it. In the traditional learning environment the instructor arranges instruction to maximize learning. He organizes information in a way that helps students remember it; he gives examples and points out critical features of concepts and principles to help the students understand them. The instructor decides which questions to ask to help the learner comprehend the text or to solve a complex problem. Students do not have to generate their own learning strategies; the teacher does it for them. The assumption has been that during the course of schooling, people will acquire most of the basic knowledge and skills they will ever need. Little attention has been given to teaching students how to learn.

These assumptions of the past are no longer tenable. Rapid advances in technology are creating such an explosion of new information that adults must continue to learn long after they have completed their formal schooling. They must acquire new knowledge to keep up with changes in their jobs, or to shift to new ones; in their everyday lives they must cope with new products generated by technology. It is impossible to teach students in school all of the basic knowledge they will need in later life. Thus, students must learn how to learn, how to acquire new knowledge, and how to approach and solve problems they have never before encountered. Now, more than ever, it is important to teach the processes of learning, in addition to knowledge.

In both of these learning components, acquiring knowledge and learning how to acquire it, the environment is structured and, for the most part, teacher-directed. In the traditional environment, learning is apt to be highly structured and tightly controlled by the instructor. In the learning-to-learn environment the student assumes more of the responsibility, while the instructor's role changes to that of guide and helper, rather than sole leader. Nevertheless, the instructor's role continues to be an important one. The instructor still sets goals for the student, makes those goals known to her, and helps her attain them.

In a totally different, third environment, the student is in control and learning is unstructured. The student's curiosity and creativity are allowed free rein. The teacher is a resource for the student to draw on when she chooses. There are no preset goals; the student is supposed to set her own.

The computer has been used in all three learning environments.

CAI and Learning Environments

A major emphasis in this text has been on the computer as a system for delivering knowledge. Obviously, people need to acquire basic knowledge in order to function in society and to advance in thinking. This basic knowledge should be transmitted as quickly and efficiently, and in as interesting and insightful a way, as possible. The computer can help to perform this task. Society would make little progress if every person had to discover for himself all that is known today; it makes far more sense to learn what is already known and build on that. A second reason for the emphasis here on the teaching of knowledge is that, inadequate as it is, more is known about instructional design for that purpose than for others.

It has also been emphasized that learning to learn is equally important, and that the computer is a viable and unique tool for that purpose. Unfortunately, we know as yet relatively little about how to help students learn how to learn, either on or off the computer. To design such instruction we need a better understanding of students' learning processes and information about which learning skills they are lacking. One way to accomplish this goal is to observe students' learning processes as they attempt to learn new concepts. We can then design instruction based on these observations. The computer can be a tool to help us monitor and study those processes.

The computer can serve an additional instructional function. It can be a tool for learning a new way of thinking and learning. For example, a new and constructive way of thinking about an error is that an error is not something to be embarrassed about but rather something to be "debugged." If the student writes a computer program to draw a flower, and the program does not draw the flower as anticipated, the student is not wrong. He simply has a "bug" and must find ways to resolve the problem. This approach is exciting and creative. However, it is not clear whether some of its fundamental premises are valid.

One assumption is that computers can affect the way children think. We don't know if this is true; there are no data either to support the assumption or to reject it. Students may learn a new way of thinking about programming yet not make a transfer to other content domains. A second assumption is that children are capable of setting their own goals, and a third, that they want to do so. The limited data that are available do not support these assumptions. One study of the instructional function of commercial microprocessor games reveals that "Children did not care to be able to create their own equations or games. When presented with such a situation, children invariably worried and asked for instruction. 'What should I put in here, sir?' became a familiar refrain" (EPIE, 1981). It may be that the children did not know how to set their own goals because they had never been allowed to do so. It may also be that not everybody can be that creative, or at least not creative enough in this subject matter area.

This is not to suggest that this creative approach should be discarded just because we cannot predict a priori what children will learn. If we do not try it, we will never know. However, it is best not to have too many expectations until more data are provided; it cannot be assumed that what "might be" is an established fact. We may find that this approach to learning how to learn must be modified in order to be effective.

Using the computer as a tool of instruction rather than as a deliverer might be more educationally effective if goals were set for the students by the instructors, at least initially. Setting goals does not necessarily take away creativity. It points the student in a given direction and enables him to judge when he has achieved the goal. Moshell (1980) has done just that in a curriculum that teaches students some basic programming and problem-solving concepts in computer science. Students create cartoon characters and program the characters to perform certain functions. The student is not left to set his own goals; instead, the teacher sets them for him. The teacher knows which concepts the student has to learn, such as the concept of a loop in programming. The teacher asks questions to orient the student to the goal. The student answers the questions and learns the concept, not from reading a definition, but by writing a program that employs this concept in a highly visible way, a way that is interpretable by the student. When the student programs a loop that moves his cartoon figure in a nonstopping fashion on the display, he can see for himself the meaning of a loop; he can see that if he wants his figure to stop, he has to write that information into his program. Here, too, we do not know if what the student *can* learn is what he *does* learn. However, the conditions of learning here are such that there is a high probability that learning does occur.

Conclusion

An eclectic approach to CAI is recommended. Our responsibility is two-fold: to help people learn and to help them learn how to learn. Instructional design based on a planned approach and on the experience and research of others has the highest probability of immediate results of educational significance. However, we must not limit ourselves to what is known; we must also try new approaches to the uses of computers in instruction. These new approaches should be carefully monitored to determine exactly how they are effective, for whom they are effective, and how they can influence the learning process.

Bibliography

Aiken, R. M. Observations on teaching a graduate course in computer assisted instruction/ computer managed instruction. *Journal of Computer-Based Instruction,* 1975, *2,* 30-25.

Alderman, D. L. *Evaluation of the TICCIT computer-assisted instructional system in the community college,* Final Report, R 78-10. Princeton, NJ: Educational Testing Service, 1978.

Anderson, R. C., & Kulhavy, R. W. Learning concepts from definitions. *American Educational Research Journal,* 1972, *9,* 385-390.

Anderson, R. C., & Faust, G. W. *Educational psychology.* New York: Harper & Row, 1973.

Arenson, M. Guidelines for the development of computer-assisted instruction materials in music theory. In *Proceedings of the Association for the Development of Computer-based Instructional Systems* (ADCIS). Bellingham, WA: ADCIS, 1977, 101-103.

Arenson, M. A model for systematic revision of computer-based instruction materials in music theory. *Journal of Computer-Based Instruction,* 1981, *7,* 78-83.

Avner, E. S. Computer-assisted instruction in astronomy. *Journal of College Science Teaching,* 1972, *1-4,* 44-46.

Avner, E. S. Teaching the sky by computer. *Mercury,* 1974, Nov/Dec, 30-31.

Avner, R. A. *An evaluation-oriented approach to production of computer-based instructional material (CERL Report X-33).* Urbana, IL: University of Illinois, 1972. (ERIC Document Reproduction Service No. ED 124 135).

Avner, R. A. *Prototype reporting format for curriculum lesson development.* Unpublished manuscript. Urbana, IL: University of Illinois, 1973.

Avner, R. A. How to produce ineffective CAI material. *Educational Technology,* 1974, *14,* 26-27.

Avner, R. A. Production of computer based materials. In H. F. O'Neill, Jr., (Ed.), *Issues in instructional development.* New York: Academic Press, 1979.

Baker, E. L., Herman, J. L., & Yeh, J. P. Fun and games: Their contribution to basic skills instruction in elementary school. *American Educational Research Journal,* 1981, *18,* 83-92.

Bitzer, M. D., Boudreaux, M., & Avner, R. A. *Computer-based instruction of basic nursing utilizing inquiry approach* (CERL Report X-40). Urbana, IL: Computer-based Education Research Laboratory, University of Illinois, 1973.

Block, J. H., & Tierney, M. L. An exploration of two correction procedures used in mastery learning approaches to instruction. *Journal of Educational Psychology,* 1974, *66,* 962–967.

Bloom, B. S. Affective outcomes of school learning. *Phi Delta Kappan,* 1977, *59,* 193–198.

Bloom, B. S., Hastings, J. T., & Madaus, G. F. *Handbook on formative and summative evaluation of student learning.* New York: McGraw-Hill, 1971.

Blumenfeld, G. J., Taylor, T., Newman, I., & Johnson, A. Relationship of college students' study skills and locus of control orientation with achievement in a self-paced computer managed course of instruction. In *Proceedings of the Association for the Development of Computer-based Instructional Systems* (ADCIS). Bellingham, WA: ADCIS, 1979, 811–823.

Bork, A. Computers as an aid to increasing physical intuition. *American Journal of Physics,* 1978, *46,* 796–800.

Boysen, V. A., Thomas, R. A., & Mortenson, W. P. Interactive computer simulation of reading skill weakness. *Journal of Computer-Based Instruction,* 1979, *5,* 45–49.

Bransford, J. D., Nitsch, K. E., & Franks, J. J. Schooling and the facilitation of knowing. In R. C. Anderson, R. J. Spiro, & W. E. Montague (Eds.), *Schooling and the acquisition of knowledge.* Hillsdale, N.J.: Lawrence Erlbaum Associates, 1977.

Brenner, L. P., & Kraatz, J. *The evaluation of PLATO instructional simulations.* Paper presented at the Annual Meeting of the American Educational Research Association, San Francisco, 1979. (ERIC Document Reproduction Service No. ED 195 248).

Briggs, L. J. (Ed.) *Instructional design.* Englewood Cliffs, NJ: Educational Technology Publications, 1977.

Burton, R. R., & Brown, J. S. A tutoring and student modelling paradigm for gaming environments. *Computer Science and Education, Joint SIGCUE – SIGCSE Bulletin.* New York: Association for Computing Machinery, 1976.

Call-Himwich, E., & Steinberg, E. R. *Myth and reality: Essential decisions in computer-based instructional design (MTC Report No. 18).* Urbana, IL: Computer-based Educational Research Laboratory, University of Illinois, 1977. (ERIC Document Reproduction Service No. ED 152 239).

Case, R. A developmentally based theory and technology of instruction. *Review of Educational Research,* 1978, *48,* 439–463.

Chabay, R., & Smith, S. G. The use of computer-based chemistry lessons. *Journal of Chemical Education,* 1977, *54,* 745–747.

Corbet, A. T., Killam, R. N., & Gracey, M. O. An effective model for lesson design in music CAI. In *Proceedings of the Association for the Development of Computer-based Instructional Systems* (ADCIS). Bellingham, WA: ADCIS, 1981, 226–231.

Culley, G. R. *Two-pronged error analysis from computer-based instruction in Latin.* Paper presented at the Delaware Symposium on Language Studies, 1979. (ERIC Document Reproduction Service No. 193 940).

Curtin, C., Avner, R. A., & Provenzano, N. Computer-based analysis of individual learning characteristics. In R. S. Hart (Ed.), *Studies in language learning* (Vol. 3). Urbana, IL: Language Learning Laboratory, University of Illinois, 1981.

Curtin, C. M., Dawson, C. L., Provenzano, N., & Cooper, P. The PLATO system: Using the computer to teach Russian. *Slavic and East European Journal,* 1976, *20,* 280–292.

Dare, F. C. *Evaluation of the PLATO IV system in a military training environment* (Vol. 1). Aberdeen Proving Ground, MD: U.S. Army Ordinance Center and School, 1975.

Downing, B. D., & Lowe, N. Mathematics anxiety and performance with CAI. In *Proceedings of the Association for the Development of Computer-based Instructional Systems* (ADCIS). Bellingham, WA: ADCIS, 1981, 45–50.

Dwyer, F. M. Adapting visual illustrations for effective learning. *Harvard Educational Review,* 1967, *37,* 250–263.

Dwyer, F. M., & Arnold, T. A. The instructional effect of verbal/visual feedback in visualized instruction. *The Journal of Psychology,* 1976, *94,* 36–41.

Educational Products Information Exchange. *Microcomputer coursework/Microprocessor games.* Stony Brook, NY: State University of New York at Stony Brook, 1981.

Fisher, M. D., Blackwell, L. R., Garcia, A. B., & Greene, J. C. Effects of student control and choice on engagement in a CAI arithmetic task in a low-income school. *Journal of Educational Psychology,* 1975, *67,* 776–783.

Faust, G. W. Fixed design strategy and the TICCIT system. *Viewpoints,* 1974, *50,* 91–101.

Flake, J. L. Interactive computer simulations for teacher education. *Educational Technology,* 1975, *15*(3), 54–57.

Francis, L. D. Computer-simulated qualitative inorganic chemistry. *Journal of Chemical Education,* 1973, *50,* 556–557.

Francis, L. Factors contributing to success in author training. In *Proceedings of the Association for the Development of Computer-based Instructional Systems* (ADCIS). Bellingham, WA: ADCIS, 1977, 192–195.

Francis, L., Goldstein, M., & Sweeney, E. *Lesson review. (MTC Report No. 3).* Urbana, IL: Computer-based Education Research Laboratory, University of Illinois, 1975. (ERIC Document Reproduction Service No. ED 124 132).

Francis, L., & Weaver, T. *Analysis of student interaction data from CBE lesssons. (MTC Report No. 15).* Urbana, IL: Computer-based Education Research Laboratory, University of Illinois, 1977. (ERIC Document Reproduction Service No. 152 237).

Frase, L. T. Advances in research and theory in instructional technology. In F. N. Kerlinger (Ed.), *Review of research in education* (Vol. 3). Itasca, IL: F. E. Peacock, 1975.

Frase, L. T., & Schwartz, B. J. Typographical cues that facilitate comprehension. *Journal of Educational Psychology,* 1979, *71,* 197–206.

Fry, J. P. Interactive relationship between inquisitiveness and student control of instruction. *Journal of Educational Psychology,* 1972, *63,* 459–465.

Gagne, R. M. *The conditions of learning* (3rd ed.). New York: Holt, Rinehart & Winston, 1977.

Gagne, R. M., & Briggs, L. J. *Principles of instructional design.* New York: Holt, Rinehart & Winston, 1974.

Gerhold, G. A., & King, D. M. Computer-simulated qualitative analysis without flowsheets. *Journal of Computer-Based Instruction,* 1974, *1,* 46–49.

Glaser, R., & Resnick, L. B. Instructional psychology. In P. H. Mussen & M. R. Rosenzweig (Eds.), *Annual Review of Psychology,* 1972, *23,* 207–276.

Glaser, R. Components of a psychology of instruction: Toward a science of design. *Review of Educational Research,* 1976, *46,* 1–24. (a)

Glaser, R. Cognitive psychology and instructional design. In D. Klahr (Ed.), *Cognition and instruction.* Hillsdale, NJ: Lawrence Erlbaum Associates, 1976. (b)

Gotkin, L. G. Programmed instruction as a strategy for developing curricula for disadvantaged children. *Monographs of the Society for Research in Child Development,* 1968, *33*(8), 19–35.

Grimes, G. M., Burke, T. J. North, L., & Friedman, J. Diagnosing simulated clinical cases using a computer-based education system. *Journal of Veterinary Medical Education,* 1974, *1,* 18–20.

Gronlund, N. E. *Measurement and evaluation in teaching.* New York: Macmillan, 1976.

Handler, P., & Sherwood, J. The PLATO system population dynamics course. In P. Reining & I. Timker (Eds.), *Population dynamics.* New York: Academic Press, 1972.

Hart, R. S. Language study and the PLATO system. In R. S. Hart (Ed.), *Studies in language learning* (Vol. 3). Urbana, IL: Language Learning Laboratory, University of Illinois, 1981.

Hartnett, R. T. Adult learners and new faculty roles. *Findings,* 1974, *1*(3), 1–8.

Heal, J. J., Jr., & O'Neil, H. F., Jr. Reduction of state anxiety via instructional design in computer-based learning environments. In J. E. Sieber, H. F. O'Neil, Jr., & S. Tobias

(Eds.), *Anxiety, learning, and instruction.* Hillsdale, NJ: Lawrence Erlbaum Associates, 1977.

Heck, W. P., Johnson, J., & Kansky, R. J. *Guidelines for evaluating instructional materials.* Reston, VA: National Council of Teachers of Mathematics, 1981.

Hofstetter, F. J. Interactive simulation/games as an aid to musical learning. In *Proceedings of the Association for the Development of Computer-based Instructional Systems* (ADCIS). Bellingham, WA: ADCIS, 1977, 104–117.

Hyatt, G., Eades, D., & Tenczar, P. Computer-based education in biology. *Bio Science,* 1972, 401–409.

Jones, M. C. TICCIT applications in higher education: Evaluation results. In *Proceedings of the Association for the Development of Computer-based Instructional Systems* (ADCIS). Bellingham, WA: ADCIS, 1978, 398–406.

Judd, W. A., Bunderson, C. V., & Bessent, E. W. *An investigation of the effects of learner control in computer-assisted instruction prerequisite mathematics (MATHS Tech. Rep. 5).* Austin, Texas: University of Texas. (ERIC Document Reproduction Service No. ED 053 532).

Kachru, Y., Nelson, C., & Hart, R. Computer-based instruction in elementary Hindi. In R. S. Hart (Ed.), *Studies in language learning* (Vol. 3). Urbana, IL: Language Learning Laboratory, University of Illinois, 1981.

Klausmeier, H. J., Ghatola, E. S., & Frayer, D. A. *Conceptual learning and development, a cognitive view.* New York: Academic Press, 1974.

Kulhavy, R. W. Feedback in written instructon. *Review of Educational Research,* 1977, *47,* 211–232.

Kulhavy, R. W., & Anderson, R. C. Delay-retention effect with multiple-choice tests. *Journal of Educational Psychology,* 1972, *63,* 505–572.

Lahey, G. F. The effect of instructional sequence on performance in computer-based instruction. *Journal of Computer-Based Instruction,* 1981, *7,* 111–116.

Logan, R. S. A state-of-the-art assessment of instructional systems development. In H. F. O'Neil, Jr. (Ed.), *Issues in instructional systems development.* New York: Academic Press, 1979.

Mager, R. F. *Preparing instructional objectives* (2nd ed.). Belmont, CA: Pitman Learning, 1975.

Malone, T. W. What makes things fun to learn? Palo Alto, CA: Xerox Corporation Palo Alto Research Center, 1980.

Markle, S. M. They teach concepts, don't they? *Educational Researcher,* 1975, *4,* 3–9.

Markle, S. M. *Designs for instructional designers.* Champaign, IL: Stipes Publishing, 1978.

Marty, F. Reflections on the use of computers in second language acquisition. In R. S. Hart (Ed.), *Studies in language learning* (Vol. 3). Urbana, IL: Language Learning Laboratory, University of Illinois, 1981.

Mayer, R. E. Information processing variables in learning to solve problems. *Review of Educational Research,* 1975, *45,* 525–541.

Mayer, R. E., & Green, J. G. Structural differences between learning outcomes produced by different instructional methods. *Journal of Educational Psychology,* 1972, *63,* 165–173.

McKeachie, W. J. Instructional psychology. In M. R. Rosenzweig & L. W. Porter (Eds.), *Annual Review of Psychology,* 1974, *25,* 161–193.

McPherson-Turner, C. CAI readiness checklist: Formative author-evaluation of CAI lessons. *Journal of Computer-Based Instruction,* 1979, *6,* 47–49.

Merrill, M. D., & Boutwell, R. C. Instructional development: Methodology and research. In F. N. Kerlinger (Ed.), *Review of research in education.* Itasca, IL: F . E. Peacock, 1973.

Merrill, P. F. *Training personnel for the Florida PLATO projects.* Paper presented at the Annual Meeting of the American Educational Research Association, Washington, D.C., 1975.

(ERIC Document Reproduction Service No. ED 105 860).

Montague, W. E. *Design considerations in computer-based instructional development systems.* Paper presented at the Annual Meeting of the American Educational Research Association, San Francisco, April 1979. (ERIC Document Reproduction Service No. ED 172 766).

Montanelli, R. G., Jr., & Steinberg, E. R. Evaluation of CS lessons. In J. Nievergelt (Ed.), *ACSES: An automated computer science education system at the University of Illinois.* (Report UIUCDCS-R-76-810). Urbana, Department of Computer Science, University of Illinois, 1976.

Moshell, J. M., Amann, G. W., & Baird, W. E. Structured gaming: Play and work in high school computer science. In *Proceedings of NECC/2.* Iowa City, University of Iowa, 1980, 266–270.

Nichols, R. D., & Wilson, J. H. The computer display as a medium in the teaching of aesthetics in visual design. In *Proceedings of the Association for the Development of Computer-based Instructional Systems* (ADCIS). Bellingham, WA: ADCIS, 1977, 248–255.

Obertino, P., Fillman, L., Gilfillan, J., & Yeager, R. *Elementary reading on PLATO IV.* Urbana, IL: Computer-based Education Research Laboratory, University of Illinois, 1977. (ERIC Document Reproduction Service No. ED 163 993).

O'Neil, J. F., Jr., & Richardson, F. C. Anxiety and learning in computer-based learning. In J. E. Sieber, H. F. O'Neil, Jr., & S. Tobias (Eds.), *Anxiety, learning, and instruction.* Hillsdale, NJ: Lawrence Erlbaum Associates, 1977.

Ottman, R. W., Killam, R. N., Adams, R. M., Bales, W. K., Bertsche, S. V., Gay, L. C., Marshall, D. B., Peak, D. A., & Ray, D. Development of a concept-centered-ear-training CAI system. *Journal of Computer-Based Instruction,* 1980, *6,* 79–86.

Papert, S. *Mindstorms.* New York: Basic Books, 1980.

Peters, H. J., & Johnson, J. W. *Author's guide.* Iowa City, University of Iowa, 1981.

Placek, R. W. A model for integrating computer-assisted instruction materials into the music curriculum. *Journal of Computer-Based Instruction,* 1980, *6,* 99–105.

Pogue, R. E., & Urban, S. D. Authoring systems, not programming languages. In *Proceedings of the Association for the Development of Computer-based Instructional Systems* (ADCIS). Bellingham, WA: ADCIS, 1981, 40–41.

Reigeluth, C. M. TICCIT to the future: Advances in instructional theory for CAI. *Journal of Computer-Based Instruction,* 1979, *6,* 40–46.

Resnick, C. A. *Computational models of learners for computer-assisted instruction.* Unpublished doctoral dissertation, University of Illinois at Urbana-Champaign, 1975.

Resnick, L. B. Task analysis in instructional design: Some cases from mathematics. In D. Klahr (Ed.), *Cognition and instruction.* Hillsdale, NJ: Lawrence Erlbaum Associates, 1976.

Richardson, J. J. The limits of frame-based CAI. In *Proceedings of the Association for the Development of Computer-based Instructional Systems* (ADCIS). Bellingham, WA: ADCIS, 1981, 88–94.

Roe, M. H., & Aiken, R. M. A CAI simulation program for teaching IRT techniques. *Journal of Computer-Based Instruction,* 1976, *2,* 52–56.

Rothbart, A., & Steinberg, E. R. Some observations of children's reactions to computer-assisted instruction. *Arithmetic Teacher,* 1971, 19–21.

Rubin, H., Geller, J., & Hanks, J. Computer simulation as a teaching tool in biology. *Journal of Computer-Based Instruction,* 1977, *3,* 91–96.

Sandman, R. S., & Welch, W. W. *Evaluation of Title I CAI programs at Minnesota correctional institutions, 1978.* (ERIC Document Reproduction Service No. ED 189 125).

Scanlan, R. T. Computer-assisted Instruction in Latin. *Classical Journal,* 1971, *66,* 223–227.

Scanlan, R. T. A computer assisted instructional course in vocabulary building through Latin and Greek roots. *Foreign Language Annals,* 1976, 579–583.

Schallert, D. L. The role of illustrations in reading comprehension. In R. J. Spiro, B. C. Bruce, & W. F. Brewer (Eds.), *Theoretical issues in reading comprehension.* Hillsdale, NJ: Lawrence Erlbaum Associates, 1980.

Schuyler, J. A. Computer augmentation of the CAI courseware authoring process—the CAI design system. *Journal of Computer-Based Instruction*, 1976, *3*, 59–67.

Schuyler, J. A. The demise of the programmer. In *Proceedings of the Association for the Development of Computer-based Instructional Systems* (ADCIS). Bellingham, WA: ADCIS, 1979, 863–869.

Seiler, B. A., & Weaver, C. S. *Description of PLATO whole number arithmetic lessons.* Urbana, IL: Computer-based Education Research Laboratory, University of Illinois, 1976.

Skavavil, R. V. Computer-based instruction of introductory statistics. *Journal of Computer-Based Instruction*, 1974, *1*, 32–30.

Smith, S. G., & Chabay, R. Computer games in chemistry. *Journal of Chemical Education*, 1977, *54*, 688–689.

Spielberger, C. D. Computer-based research on anxiety and learning: An overview and critique. In J. E. Sieber, H. E. O'Neil, Jr., & S. Tobias (Eds.), *Anxiety, learning, and instruction.* Hillsdale, NJ: Lawrence Erlbaum Associates, 1977.

Steinberg, E. R. *Educational guide.* (PLATO Evaluation Note, 1-11). Urbana, IL: Computer-based Education Research Laboratory, University of Illinois, 1974.

Steinberg, E. R. *The evolutionary design of CAI courseware.* Paper presented at Annual Meeting of American Educational Research Association, 1975. (ERIC Document Reproduction Service No. ED 105 888).

Steinberg, E. R. Review of student control in computer-assisted instruction. *Journal of Computer-Based Instruction*, 1977, *3*, 84–90.

Steinberg, E. R. Learner interaction in computer-assisted instruction. In *Proceedings of the Association for the Development of Computer-based Instructional Systems* (ADCIS). Bellingham, WA: ADCIS, 1979, 194–202.

Steinberg, E. R. Evaluation processes in young children's problem-solving. *Contemporary Educational Psychology*, 1980, *5*, 276–281. (a)

Steinberg, E. R. *Experience vs two kinds of feedback in CAI problem solving.* Urbana, IL: Computer-based Education Research Laboratory, University of Illinois, 1980. (ERIC Document Reproduction Service No. ED 194 076). (g)

Steinberg, E. R. Problem complexity and the transfer of strategies in computer-presented problems. *American Educational Research Journal*, 1983, *20*, 13–28.

Steinberg, E. R., Avner, R. A., Call-Himwich, E., Francis, L., Himwich, A., Klecka, J. A., & Misselt, A. L. *Critical incidents in the evolution of PLATO projects. (MTC Report No. 12).* Urbana, IL: Computer-based Education Research Laboratory, University of Illinois, 1977. (ERIC Document Reproduction Service No. ED 148 298).

Suppes, P., & Morningstar, M. *Computer-assisted instruction at Stanford, 1966–68: Data, models, and evaluation of the arithmetic programs.* New York: Academic Press, 1972.

Tennyson, R. D. The role of evaluation in instructional development. *Educational Technology*, 1976, *16*, 17–24.

Tennyson, R. D. Instructional control strategies and content structure as design variables in concept acquisition using computer-based instruction. *Journal of Educational Psychology*, 1980, *72*, 525–532.

Tennyson, R. D., & Park, O. C. The teaching of concepts: A review of instructional design research literature. *Review of Educational Research*, 1980, *50*, 55–70.

Tiemann, P. W., & Markle, S. M. *Analyzing instructional content: A guide to instruction and evaluation.* Champaign, IL: Stipes, 1978.

Tobias, S. Distraction, response mode, anxiety, and achievement in computer-assisted instruction. *Journal of Educational Psychology*, 1973, *65*, 233–237.

Tobias, S., & Duchastel, P. C. Behavioral objectives, sequence, and anxiety in CAI. *Instructional Science*, 1974, *3*, 231–242.

Trollip, S. R. *System performance and student evaluation in a complex computer-based procedural training program.* Technical Report ARL-75-4/AF OSR-75-1. 1975 Air Force Office of Scientific Research U.S. Air Force.

Weaver, C. A., & Seiler, B. A. Computer assistance in the social processes of learning. In *Proceedings of the Association for the Development of Computer-based Instructional Systems* (ADCIS). Bellingham, WA: ADCIS, 1977, 26–38.

Wilson, J., & Paden, E. The effects of drill structure on learning in phonetics lessons. In *Proceedings of the Association for the Development of Computer-based Instructional Systems* (ADCIS). Bellingham, WA: ADCIS, 1978, 448–456.

Wittrock, M. C. The cognitive movement in instruction. *Educational Researcher,* 1979, *8,* 5–11.

Wittrock, M. C., & Lumsdaine, A. A. Instructional psychology. In M. R. Rosenzweig & L. W. Porter (Eds.), *Annual Review of Psychology,* 1977, *28,* 417– 459.

Yeager, R. F. CMI and the logical analysis of curriculum. In *Proceedings of the Association for the Development of Computer-based Instructional Systems* (ADCIS). Bellingham, WA: ADCIS, 1977, 55–60.

Index